IRELAND

D1236165

Isabel Albiston, Brian Barry, Yvonne Gordon, Úna-Minh Kavanagh,
Noelle Kelly, Fionán McGrath, Orla Smith & Neil Arthurs

Contents

Discover Gaelic culture and celebrate ancient Celtic festivals. Follow in the footsteps of literary greats. Hike along the coast, splash in the sea and kayak around peaceful loughs. Take the scenic route through moody mountains. Feel exhilarated by soaring sea cliffs, pristine beaches and the wild Atlantic Ocean. Spot nesting seabirds and marine mammals. Sip pints of creamy stout. Feast on fresh local produce. Tap your feet to trad music. See the North's complicated history reflected on its painted walls.

This is Ireland.

TURN THE PAGE AND START PLANNING YOUR NEXT BEST TRIP →

Above Waterville, Kerry

IRISH LANGUAGE STATS

The total population of the Gaeltacht is 96,090.

In Ireland 73,803 people speak Irish daily.

The county with the highest percentage of Irish speakers is Galway (49%).

GAELIC
CULTURE

Gaelic culture encompasses the Irish language, literature, storytelling and folklore, Irish dancing and trad music, Gaelic sports, traditional arts and crafts, and the celebration of ancient Celtic festivals. In certain areas of the country, Gaelic culture thrives: locals regularly speak Irish, pubs buzz with trad sessions, and hurling and Gaelic football are part of community life. The best way to experience Gaelic culture is to visit a Gaeltacht (Irish-speaking region).

→ THE GAELIC REVIVAL

The 19th-century Gaelic revival was a resurgence of interest in the Irish language, literature, folklore and sports. A key proponent was WB Yeats.

Left Sign indicating a Gaelic-speaking area, Galway **Right** Irish poet WB Yeats **Below** Camogie match, Cork

FESTIVALS

Ancient Celtic festivals such as Imbolc (the beginning of spring) are still celebrated across Ireland. Rituals include mountain pilgrimages, parties and parades.

↑ GAELIC SPORTS

The Gaelic Athletic Association (GAA) promotes Ireland's Gaelic games of hurling and Gaelic football, as well as camogie, handball and rounders.

Best Gaelic Culture Experiences

▶ Watch hurling being played or have a go yourself. (p112)

▶ Join the festivities at one of Ireland's ancient Celtic celebrations. (p162)

▶ Hear trad music in Galway's pubs. (p186)

▶ Learn about Gaelic culture in Dublin's museums. (p72)

▶ Visit the Irish-speaking Gaeltacht of Corca Dhuibhne (Dingle Peninsula; p153) and the Donegal Gaeltacht (p229).

↘ **CRAFT STOUTS**

Blacks Brewery
World's End

Burren Brewery
Burren Black

Galway Bay Brewery Buried at Sea

Lineman Astral Grains Foreign Extra Stout

Porterhouse Around the Clock Imperial Stout

STOUT OF
ORDER

▬▬ For many, experiencing Ireland means finding out for themselves whether Guinness really tastes better in its native land. While Guinness has become synonymous with stout, in Ireland Murphy's and Beamish also compete for business. It's no surprise that stouts are also something of a speciality among Ireland's craft brewers.

Best Beer Experiences

▶ Search out the perfect pint in Dublin, where Guinness is brewed. (p52)

▶ Order a Murphy's with your meal in Cork. (p128)

▶ Sample stout on a Galway pub crawl. (p186)

▶ Top off a Dingle adventure with a pint of the black stuff. (p164)

ALEXANDRA-IW1977SN/ITERSTOCK ©

CONTEMPORARY IRISH FICTION

Sally Rooney
Conversations with Friends (2017)

Colm Tóibín
Brooklyn (2009)

Eimear McBride
A Girl is a Half-Formed Thing (2013)

Naoise Dolan
Exciting Times (2020)

Best Literary Experiences

▶ Visit the County Derry locations that inspired Seamus Heaney's poetry. (p222)

▶ Explore Ireland's literary connections in Dublin at the MoLI and Dublin Writers Museum. (p72)

▶ Discover the isolated beauty of Kerry's Great Blasket Island, depicted in books by three islanders. (p158)

POETS & SCHOLARS

Listen to Irish people speak and you'll hear a distinct rhythm and an often poetic turn of phrase. Ireland's strong tradition of storytelling is reflected in its remarkable literary output, which includes works by James Joyce, Oscar Wilde, WB Yeats, Samuel Beckett and Seamus Heaney.

THRILLS &
SPILLS

What better way to experience Ireland's wild beauty than to embrace the great outdoors? Options for activities abound. Follow waymarked hiking trails up mountains, over blanket bog and along the coast, cycle traffic-free greenways and mountain bike through woodland, splash in the ocean, jump on a surfboard or kayak around Ireland's peaceful loughs. Family-friendly fun is guaranteed.

→ HIKING

The Ireland Way (the irelandway.ie) is a 1000km walking trail from County Cork to the Antrim coast. Further trails are listed on sportireland.ie/outdoors and walkni.com.

Left Surfer, Mullaghmore Right Rope bridge, Carrick-a-Rede Below Cyclists, Killarney National Park

SURFING

One of the world's biggest waves breaks at Mullaghmore in County Sligo. In 2020, Irish surfer Conor Maguire surfed towering 18m-high waves here.

↑ CYCLING

The Atlantic Coast Route (atlanticonbike.ie) passes through some wild and rugged landscapes in the north-west. Many forest parks have mountain bike trails.

Best Active Experiences

▶ Leap off rocks and bob in wave pools on a Causeway Coast coasteering session. (p226)

▶ Kayak or canoe out to Lough Erne's monastic islands. (p216)

▶ Hike the beautiful Kerry Camino. (p156)

▶ Surf the wild Atlantic waves off the coast of County Sligo. (p222)

▶ Cycle the Waterford Greenway at the Copper Coast. (p116)

ONES TO WATCH

Red deer Roam the hillsides of the Wicklow Mountains and Glenveagh National Park.

Dolphins, porpoises and whales Can be spotted off the coast.

Puffins Nest in colonies on coastal cliffs.

Breeding seabirds Include gannets, kittiwakes and fulmars.

WILDLIFE
WONDERS

Ireland's land mammals are fairly low-key; they include hares, hedgehogs and red deer. When it comes to wildlife watching, it's the visiting species that draw the crowds. Nesting seabirds include remarkable colonies of puffins, while Ireland is also a stopover for migrating birds. Minke whales can be spotted off the west coast in the summer, followed by fin whales and humpback whales later in the year.

→ **BIRD SPOTTING**

Spring and autumn are the seasons to spot migratory birds (mainly waders and warblers) on their way to and from the Arctic, Africa and North America.

Left Red deer, Glenveagh National Park **Right** Razorbill **Below** Round-leaved sundew

MARINE MAMMALS

The Irish Whale and Dolphin Group (iwdg.ie) records sightings and campaign for Irish waters to be declared a whale and dolphin sanctuary.

↑ **BOG LIFE**

Ireland's areas of blanket bog – particularly prevalent in Counties Mayo and Donegal – support a rich diversity of plant and animal species.

Best Wildlife Experiences

▶ **Spot whales and dolphins from Mizen Head in County Cork. (p130)**

▶ **Look out for falcons, golden eagles and red deer in Glenveagh National Park. (p230)**

▶ **Admire the abundant flora and fauna of the Burren. (p194)**

▶ **Observe seabirds at Little Skellig, the Kerry island that's a birdwatching haven. (p158)**

▶ **Take a ferry to the Saltees, where an abundance of seabirds nest. (p107)**

IRELAND'S NATIONAL PARKS

Ballycroy
County Mayo

The Burren
County Clare

Connemara
County Galway

Glenveagh
County Donegal

Killarney
County Kerry

Wicklow Mountains
County Wicklow

THE SCENIC
ROUTE

The Irish landscape can be both brooding and breathtakingly beautiful. The country's spectacular coastline gets the most attention, but Ireland's moody mountains, rolling green pastures and atmospheric loughs and rivers are evocative in their own way. Changeable weather adds to the allure: low-lying mists and pretty sunsets bring a touch of romance.

→ DARK SKIES

Ballycroy National Park is a designated Dark Sky Park (mayodarkskypark.ie). From the visitor centre, a boardwalk leads to a viewpoint for spectacular stargazing.

Left Wicklow Mountains **Right** Ballycroy National Park **Below** Ring of Kerry

INLAND WATERWAYS

Taking a slow trip along Ireland's rivers and waterways allows the beauty of the country's varied landscapes to seep in.

↑ DRIVING

Negotiating winding rural roads through wild terrain while dodging sheep is all part of the experience. Ireland's signed coastal driving routes are simply spectacular.

Best Scenic Experiences

▶ Meander down the River Shannon in a boat. (p176)

▶ Admire Wicklow's elegant gardens and historic homes. (p84)

▶ Experience County Donegal's brooding mountains and wild terrain. (p228)

▶ Paddle the waterways of Lough Erne in County Fermanagh. (p216)

▶ Walk through forests, up mountains and around loughs in County Wicklow. (p92)

ICONIC
CLIFFS &
BEACHES

Ireland has one of the world's most stunning shorelines. Rugged cliffs are interspaced with secluded coves and sandy bays that are perfect for surfing. Vibrant green grass and wildflowers grow right up to the cliff edge, where sure-footed sheep graze perilously above crashing waves. On the western coast, the Wild Atlantic Way is a signed driving route from Kinsale to Derry.

Coastal Donegal
Cliffs and beaches
The Sliabh Liag cliffs are among Europe's highest. See them from the water on a guided boat trip, or brave the narrow One Man's Path along the top. Nearby are some of Ireland's most beautiful beaches. ▶ p232
🕐 *50-minute drive from Donegal town to Sliabh Liag*

Cliffs of Moher
Soaring sea cliffs
On the coast of County Clare, these magnificent cliffs stretch for 8km. Join the crowds who come to gawp in wonder. The best views are on the trail from Hag's Head, or from a boat.
▶ p188
🕐 *40-minute drive from Ennis*

Dingle Peninsula
Secluded sandy coves
Jutting into the wild Atlantic Ocean at mainland Ireland's most westerly point, the Dingle Peninsula offers craggy cliffs, surf-pounded rocks and pretty beaches. Take a hike at Dunmore Head for spectacular views over the Blasket Islands. ▶ p164
🕐 *50-minute drive from Tralee to Dingle town*

Beara Peninsula
Wild and unspoilt headland
County Cork's beguilingly rugged headland is quieter than the often crowded Ring of Kerry. For breathtaking views, take the Healy Pass across the Caha Mountains, then stop for a swim at Ballydonegan beach.
▶ p130
🕐 *2½-hour drive from Cork city to Ballydonegan beach*

Mullet Peninsula
Ballina
Castlebar
Croagh Patrick
Westport
Clifden
Galway

Loop Head

Connor Pass
Tralee
Dingle Peninsula
Dingle
Killarney

Skellig Islands

Beara Peninsula
Skibbereen

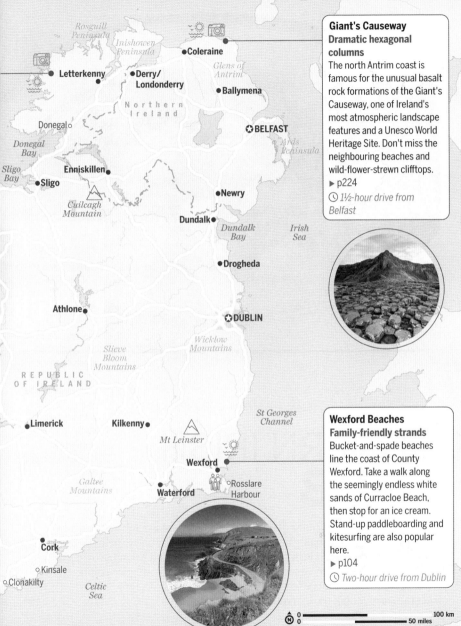

Rosguill Peninsula

Inishowen Peninsula

●Coleraine

●Letterkenny

●Derry/ Londonderry

Glens of Antrim

●Ballymena

N o r t h e r n
I r e l a n d

Donegal○

✪BELFAST

Donegal Bay

Ards Peninsula

Enniskillen●

Sligo Bay

●Sligo

Cuilcagh Mountain

●Newry

Dundalk●

Dundalk Bay

Irish Sea

●Drogheda

Athlone●

✪DUBLIN

Slieve Bloom Mountains

Wicklow Mountains

R E P U B L I C
O F   I R E L A N D

●Limerick

Kilkenny●

Mt Leinster

St Georges Channel

Wexford ●

Galtee Mountains

Waterford●

○Rosslare Harbour

●Cork

○Kinsale

○Clonakilty

Celtic Sea

Giant's Causeway
Dramatic hexagonal columns
The north Antrim coast is famous for the unusual basalt rock formations of the Giant's Causeway, one of Ireland's most atmospheric landscape features and a Unesco World Heritage Site. Don't miss the neighbouring beaches and wild-flower-strewn clifftops.
▶ p224
🕐 1½-hour drive from Belfast

Wexford Beaches
Family-friendly strands
Bucket-and-spade beaches line the coast of County Wexford. Take a walk along the seemingly endless white sands of Curracloe Beach, then stop for an ice cream. Stand-up paddleboarding and kitesurfing are also popular here.
▶ p104
🕐 Two-hour drive from Dublin

0   100 km
Ⓝ
0   50 miles

IRISH SPECIALITIES

Boxty Starchy potato cake from Ulster.

Seafood chowder Rich, creamy broth filled with the flavours of the sea.

Guinness bread Malty loaf made with the black stuff.

Irish stew Comforting bowl of meat and potatoes.

MODERN IRISH
GRUB

Ireland's thriving culinary scene is closely linked to the quality of its local produce. Swathes of lush farming country produce a bounty of meats and cheeses, while fresh seafood is available from the surrounding ocean. From gourmet sandwiches and takeaway fish-and-chips to Michelin-starred fine dining, Ireland has some excellent restaurants at all price points.

→ BALLYMALOE HOUSE

Since the 1960s, this restaurant and cookery school in Cork has been at the forefront of Ireland's local food movement. (p129)

Left Seafood chowder **Right** Jams from Ballymaloe Cooking School **Below** Cashel Blue cheese

MARKETS

Buy direct from producers at food-led markets such as St George's Market in Belfast and the weekend markets in Dublin's suburbs.

↑ LOCAL PRODUCE

Local cheeses include Cashel Blue, Corleggy and Gubbeen. In Ulster, try Armagh apples, Comber potatoes and Lough Neagh eel (if you're brave enough).

Best Food Experiences

▶ **Dine out in Kinsale, Ireland's culinary capital. (p128)**

▶ **Feast on the fruit of the land in Wicklow. (p98)**

▶ **Take your pick of options from fine-dining restaurants to food trucks in Dublin. (p52)**

▶ **Shop for local produce at the English Market in Cork. (p144)**

TRAD PLAYLIST

Old Hag You Have Killed Me
The Bothy Band

Star of County Down
The Chieftains

Dónal na Gréine
Gráinne Holland

The Wren's Nest
De Dannan

Whiskey in the Jar
The Dubliners

PINTS & TRAD
SESSIONS

Catching a trad session in an Irish pub is an experience that will long linger in your senses. From foot-tapping reels to evocative ballads, trad music creates an atmospheric soundtrack to a night out. Skilled musicians can be heard at even the most casual of venues; spend enough time there and you might even find yourself joining in.

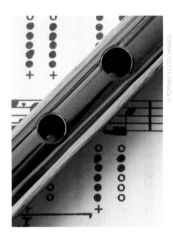

→ **TRAD INSTRUMENTS**

The uillean pipes (Irish bagpipes) are played by squeezing bellows under the elbow. Pub sessions usually feature fiddles, flutes, tin whistles, accordions and bouzoukis.

Left Trad music session, Galway **Right** Tin whistle **Below** Bodhrán

TRAD RHYTHMS

Trad music includes jigs, reels and hornpipes (which sound similar but have different timings), polkas and slow airs or ballads.

↑ **BEAT OF THE BODHRÁN**

Trad music is often accompanied by a bodhrán, a traditional Irish drum made with goatskin stretched over a wooden frame.

Best Music Experiences

▶ Join in the dancing at trad sessions on Donegal's Tory Island. (p228)

▶ Hear some of the country's best trad musicians in Galway. (p186)

▶ Tap your feet to the beat in Dingle's pubs. (p164)

▶ Whet your whistle and hear some reels on a Dublin pub crawl. (p52)

MURALS & NEW
BEGINNINGS

Ireland's turbulent history is explored in some excellent museums across the country, and provides the context for the art on display in Irish galleries and castles. In the North, echoes of past conflicts and current tensions are reflected in political murals. These days, Ireland's artistic output reflects its increasingly diverse population, and Belfast's vibrant street art scene is rooted in a non-sectarian celebration of place.

→ REVOLUTION

Dublin is the best place to learn about Ireland's revolutionary movements. It's where the most significant events took place in the fight for independence.

Left Mural by the artist 'Smug One'. Belfast **Right** GPO building, Dublin **Below** Artist and musician Patsy Dan Mac Ruairi (Rodgers), Tory Island

MURAL THEMES

Murals often depict themes connected to identity. Look for references to Celtic mythology in Republican murals and to Belfast's industrial past in Unionist murals.

Best Cultural Experiences

▶ Check out political murals and creative street art in Belfast. (p210)

▶ Immerse yourself in art at Dublin's National Museum of Ireland – Decorative Arts and History. (p72)

▶ Learn about Ireland's revolutionary movements at the GPO Museum in Dublin. (p60)

▶ Take in the striking murals of the People's Gallery in Derry. (p212)

↑ TORY ISLAND NAIVE ART

This remote island in County Donegal is known for its distinctive school of self-taught painters, whose work has been exhibited worldwide.

↓ Kilkenny Festivals

The Cat Laughs Comedy Festival in June attracts the country's top comedians; the August Arts Festival is one of Ireland's best.

▶ p204

Schools are closed in July and August. Seaside towns and resorts are busy as families head to the coast.

Avoid Northern Ireland during the Orange Order marches of 12 July (a public holiday), when tensions run high.

↑ Galway International Arts Festival

Held in the last two weeks of July, Ireland's most important arts festival features music, drama and more.

▶ giaf.ie

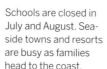

JUNE

Average daytime max: 18°C
Days of rainfall: 10

JULY

Ireland in
SUMMER

↓ All-Ireland Finals

Late summer sees the finals of the hurling and Gaelic football championships at Dublin's Croke Park.

▶ p112

↑ Galway Races

This summer festival is not just about the horses, it's also about the food, fashion and elaborate hats.

▶ Galway

▶ p204

AUGUST

Average daytime max: 20°C
Days of rainfall: 11

Average daytime max: 19°C
Days of rainfall: 12

Demand for accommodation peaks during July and August. Book tours and overnight adventures in advance at lonelyplanet.com/ireland/activities..

← Puck Fair

This ancient three-day festival takes place in August and involves the crowning of a goat king.

▶ Killorglin

▶ p162

 Packing Notes

Sandals for warm weather; trainers, a sweater and a jacket for rainy days.

Check out the full calendar of events

Though it's always unpredictable, September can be a good time to glimpse the Northern Lights from County Donegal.

← Electric Picnic

Held in early September, this three-day arts and music festival features an eclectic mix of international acts.

▶ Stradbally Hall, County Laois

▶ p204

Forage for wild blackberries and feast on local seasonal produce including mushrooms, oysters and Armagh apples.

↓ Cork Jazz Festival

The musicians spill out onto the streets at Cork's annual jazz festival, held in late October.

▶ p204

SEPTEMBER

Average daytime max: 17°C
Days of rainfall: 10

OCTOBER

Ireland in
AUTUMN

October is prime leaf-peeping time, when many trees in parks and forests turn vivid shades of red, yellow and orange.

↓ **Derry Halloween**

This annual extravaganza attracts visitors from across the globe. Events include a carnival parade and live music.

▶ derryhalloween.com

↑ **Belfast International Arts Festival**

Held in October, this huge arts festival encompasses everything from visual arts to dance.

▶ belfastinternationalartsfestival.com

Average daytime max: 14°C
Days of rainfall: 12

NOVEMBER

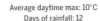

Average daytime max: 10°C
Days of rainfall: 12

Autumn is the best time for whale watching on the west coast. Look out for Minke, fin whales and humpbacks.

🧳 **Packing Notes**

A waterproof jacket and a backpack to carry extra layers in changeable weather.

Christmas dominates December: shops are busy, while pubs and restaurants host office holiday parties. On 25 December shops and businesses close.

↓ Christmas Markets

Festive Christmas markets are held in Belfast, Galway and Cork.

← Winterval

Ireland's biggest Christmas festival features a Santa's grotto, carnival games, and craft and food market stalls.

▶ Waterford

▶ winterval.ie

Falling on or around 21 December, the winter solstice is the shortest day of the year, with less than eight hours of sunlight.

DECEMBER

Average daytime max: 9°C
Days of rainfall: 13

JANUARY

Ireland in
WINTER

↓ Cultural Dublin

The winter months are a good time to explore Dublin's museums and galleries, out of the cold.

▶ p72

↑ Imbolc

Also called St Brigid's Day, 1 February marks the beginning of spring; festivities involve processions and straw hats.

▶ Killorglin
▶ p162

↓ Galway's Pubs

Ireland's pubs are cosiest in the wintertime, when short chilly days tempt you inside to sit by the fire.

▶ p186

FEBRUARY

Average daytime max: 8°C
Days of rainfall: 13

Average daytime max: 8°C
Days of rainfall: 10

← Causeway Coast

Winter is a quieter time to visit popular places such as the Giant's Causeway in County Antrim.

▶ p224

🧳 Packing Notes

A winter coat, woolly hat, scarf, gloves, warm socks and waterproof boots.

← **St Patrick's Day**

On 17 March Ireland celebrates St Patrick's Day with parades and events across the country. The biggest celebrations are in Dublin.

▶ stpatricksday.ie

The puffin breeding season usually starts in late March. From then until July or August, look out for puffins around Ireland's craggy coastline.

Hedgerows and hillsides turn bright yellow as the fragrant flower of the gorse bush blooms.

Summer festivities begin with events on the May Bank Holiday (the first Monday in May).

MARCH

Average daytime max: 12°C
Days of rainfall: 11

APRIL

Ireland in
SPRING

→ May the 4th Festival

Kerry's connection to *Star Wars* is celebrated with recitals of the score and Irish dancing.
▶ Baile an Fheirtéaraigh (Ballyferriter)
▶ p168

↓ North West 200

This huge motorcycle racing event takes place in May in the triangle between Portrush, Portstewart and Coleraine on the Causeway Coast.
▶ northwest200.org

→ Kerry Camino

Join the annual group walk of the Kerry Camino on the holiday weekend in early May.
▶ Tralee
▶ p156

MAY

Average daytime max: 15°C
Days of rainfall: 11

Average daytime max: 15°C
Days of rainfall: 11

← The Burren

May is the best time to see the wild-flowers in bloom on a walk in the Burren.
▶ County Clare
▶ p192

 Packing Notes

Trainers, light layers, a scarf, a waterproof jacket and sunglasses for bright days.

AROUND DUBLIN
Trip Builder

TAKE YOUR PICK OF MUST-SEES AND HIDDEN GEMS

Ireland's capital city offers world-class dining, culture and nightlife. But within an hour's drive of the metropolis lie peaceful mountain passes, brooding loughs and pretty seaside towns. Pack for a night out on the town, a mountain hike and a day at the beach.

🗺 Trip Notes

Hub town Dublin

How long Allow a week

Getting around Public transport within Dublin is excellent, and preferable to negotiating the city's traffic and parking challenges. The DART runs to Bray, Dalkey and Howth. Buses connect main towns, but don't serve all rural areas. It's easiest to reach the Wicklow Mountains by car.

Tips Consider basing yourself in Dublin and visiting the surrounding sights on day trips.

Dublin
Dine out at the city's excellent restaurants and drink in Dublin's famous pubs. Allow time to visit museums and galleries. Stroll the city's elegant parks.
◷ *3-4 days*

MEATH

Leixlip ●

Celbridge ●

KILDARE

● Naas

Blessington Lake
Visit the grand stately home at Russborough House & Parklands, which has views over the picturesque Blessington Lake.
◷ *½ day*

Blessington ○

Poulaphouca Reservoir

0 ——— 10 km
0 ——— 5 miles

Dublin Airport ✈

Ireland's Eye

Howth

Howth
Stroll along the cliff path to the lighthouse, check out the castle, wander around the harbour and feast on fresh seafood.
🕐 ½ day

North Bull Island

⭘ DUBLIN

Dublin Bay

Irish Sea

Dun Laoghaire

Dalkey

Killiney ⚬

Dalkey Island

Dalkey
Take a day trip to the heritage town of Dalkey. Walking trails, refreshing sea breezes, castle ruins and forest parks await.
🕐 ½ day

DUBLIN

Killakee ⚬

⚬ Loughlinstown

Bray
Admire the gardens, views and waterfall at Powerscourt Estate. The nearby town of Bray is the starting point of the Bray Head coastal walk.
🕐 ½ day

● Bray

Enniskerry

⚬ Kilmacanogue

Greystones ●

Mt Mullaghcleevaun

Lough Dan

Vartry Reservoir

Wicklow Mountains
Climb mountains, hike through forests and glens, and marvel at Glenmacnass Waterfall. Nearby is the monastic site at Glendalough, one of Ireland's most well-known attractions.
🕐 1-2 days

WICKLOW

Glendalough ⚬

⚬ Laragh

COASTAL SOUTH-WEST
Trip Builder

TAKE YOUR PICK OF MUST-SEES AND HIDDEN GEMS

▬▬▬▬ Surf breaks, hiking trails, trad pubs, wonderful wildlife, medieval castles, Ireland's best restaurants and simply spectacular scenery: a trip to the coastlines of Counties Kerry and Cork has it all. Keep your camera handy.

🗺 Trip Notes

Hub towns Tralee, Cork

How long Around a week

Getting around The best way to experience the peninsula driving loops is behind the wheel. Public transport to remote areas is limited. Take boat tours to the islands.

Tips Boat trips to the Skelligs only operate mid-May to September, weather permitting. Numbers of visitors are limited so book well in advance.

Valentia Island
Cross the bridge to beautiful Valentia Island. Hike the loop walk at Bray Head or climb Geokaun Mountain for views of the surrounding islands.
🕑 1 day

Castlegregory

Inishtooskert

Dingle o

Annascau

Great Blasket

Inishvickillane

Valentia Island

Cahersiveen

Geokaun Mountain

Lough Curran

Skellig Michael

Scariff Island

Skellig Islands
Take a boat trip to the remote monastery on Skellig Michael, featured as Luke Skywalker's Jedi temple in *Star Wars*, and spot gannets on Little Skellig.
🕑 1 day

Dursey Island

Atlantic Ocean

N 0 — 20 km
0 — 10 miles

LIMERICK

Dingle Peninsula
Drive around Slea Head, surf or catch the sunset at the Maharees and relax in Dingle's pubs. Allow three days to hike the Kerry Camino.
🕐 *2-3 days*

Tralee●

○Castlemaine

●Mallow   Fermoy○

Lough Caragh

Lough Leane ●**Killarney**

KERRY

CORK

Killarney National Park

○Kenmare

Cork

Beara Peninsula
Drive over Healy Pass and clock the jaw-dropping views. Stop at beaches and pretty villages, and at the end of the peninsula take the cable car to Dursey Island.
🕐 *1 day*

Lauragh○

Glengarriff ○

Bantry ○

Cork
Stroll around the city, sample restaurants and visit the English Market. Take day trips to Cork's medieval castles, country houses and beaches.
🕐 *2-3 days*

Bere Island   Kilcrohane

○Ballydehob   ○Rosscarbery
○Skibbereen

○Goleen

Cape Clear Island   *Sherkin Island*

Mizen Head Peninsula
Get off the beaten track in Cork's wild west. Visit ancient stone circles and take a detour to the remote Sheep's Head Peninsula.
🕐 *1 day*

Celtic Sea

THE NORTH
Trip Builder

TAKE YOUR PICK OF MUST-SEES AND HIDDEN GEMS

▬▬▬ Head north for a mix of vibrant cities and peaceful backwaters. This trip promises opportunities to hike, cycle and kayak your way through varied scenery, with chances to better understand local history and feast on good food along the way.

🗺️ Trip Notes

Hub towns Belfast, Derry

How long Around 10 days

Getting around Hire a car in Belfast. Alternatively, buses link main towns. Cycling is an excellent option: National Cycle Route 93 connects Belfast and Derry; the Inishowen 100 is a 100-mile (160km) cycle around the peninsula; the Kingfisher Trail passes Lough Erne.

Tips The 120-mile (193km) Causeway Coastal Route is a signed driving tour from Belfast to Derry.

Glenveagh National Park
Wonder at the beauty of brooding mountains and loughs. Hike or cycle through an unspoilt landscape. Spot wildlife and take a tour of Glenveagh Castle.
🕒 1 day

Milford○

Green Island

🥾 🐾 ⛰️

Letterkenny●

D O N E G A L

○ Donegal

Lough Derg

Fermanagh

Lower Lough Erne

Lough Melvin

Lough Erne
Canoe or kayak out to the monastic islands of Lower Lough Erne. Explore the quieter waters of Upper Lough Erne. Visit the island town of Enniskillen.
🕒 1-2 days

Sligo●

🧭 Ⓝ 0 ──── 20 km
      0 ──── 10 miles

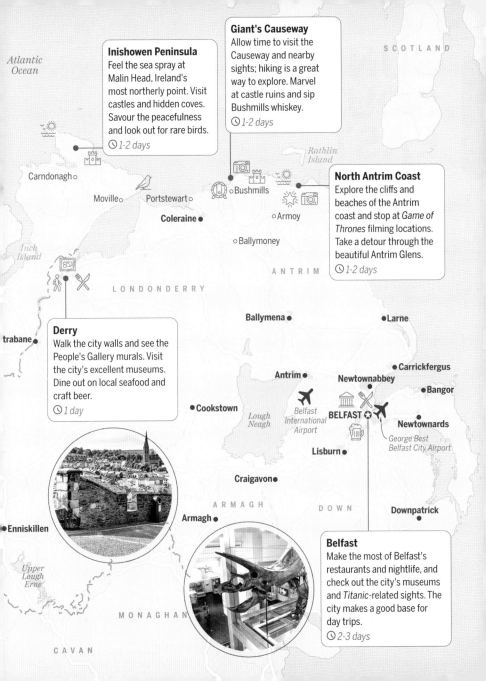

Inishowen Peninsula
Feel the sea spray at Malin Head, Ireland's most northerly point. Visit castles and hidden coves. Savour the peacefulness and look out for rare birds.
🕓 *1-2 days*

Giant's Causeway
Allow time to visit the Causeway and nearby sights; hiking is a great way to explore. Marvel at castle ruins and sip Bushmills whiskey.
🕓 *1-2 days*

SCOTLAND

Atlantic Ocean

Carndonagh o

Moville o   Portstewart o

Coleraine •

o Bushmills

Rathlin Island

o Armoy

North Antrim Coast
Explore the cliffs and beaches of the Antrim coast and stop at *Game of Thrones* filming locations. Take a detour through the beautiful Antrim Glens.
🕓 *1-2 days*

o Ballymoney

Inch Island

A N T R I M

L O N D O N D E R R Y

trabane •

Derry
Walk the city walls and see the People's Gallery murals. Visit the city's excellent museums. Dine out on local seafood and craft beer.
🕓 *1 day*

Ballymena •   • Larne

Antrim •   • Carrickfergus

Newtownabbey

• Cookstown   *Lough Neagh*   *Belfast International Airport*   • Bangor

BELFAST ✈

Newtownards

George Best Belfast City Airport

Lisburn •

• Enniskillen

Craigavon •

A R M A G H   D O W N

Armagh •   Downpatrick

Upper Lough Erne

M O N A G H A N

Belfast
Make the most of Belfast's restaurants and nightlife, and check out the city's museums and *Titanic*-related sights. The city makes a good base for day trips.
🕓 *2-3 days*

C A V A N

SUNNY SOUTH-EAST
Trip Builder

TAKE YOUR PICK OF MUST-SEES AND HIDDEN GEMS

▬▬▬ A trip to Ireland's Southeast might involve surfing, sea kayaking, cycling and walking – or simply relaxing with an ice cream on one of the sandy beaches along the coasts of Counties Wexford and Waterford. In the rolling hills of neighbouring Kilkenny are a number of family-friendly attractions.

🗺 Trip Notes

Hub towns Kilkenny, Wexford, Waterford

How long Around 4 or 5 days

Getting around Trains connect Wexford town, Waterford city and Kilkenny city with Dublin. Cycling is popular in the region. A car is the easiest option.

Tips The Passage East Ferry from Ballyhack to Passage East saves a long detour – handy if travelling along the coast between Wexford and Waterford by bike or car.

Kilkenny

○Bennettsbridge

KILKENNY

Waterford
Gawp at waterfalls, splash in the sea and stroll down sandy beaches on the Waterford coast. Cycling the Waterford Greenway is a fun excursion.
🕐 *1 day*

Booley Hills

Copper Coast
Explore the vivid landscapes of the Copper Coast Geopark. Allow time to discover the area's hidden coves and beaches. Pick up trail cards for self-guided walks.
🕐 *1 day*

Suir River

Waterford

WATERFORD

Tramore
○

Tramore Bay

Dunabrattin Head

Brownstown Head

0   10 km
Ⓝ 0   5 miles

Kilkenny

Catch a game of hurling in Kilkenny city, home of the Cats. Take the family to Castlecomer Discovery Park and other local attractions.

🕑 1 day

Wexford Beaches

Feel the sand between your toes on Wexford's beaches. In sunny weather allocate extra time for lazing on the dunes and eating ice cream.

🕑 1-2 days

Enniscorthy ●

WEXFORD

New Ross ●

Castlebridge

River Slaney

Hook Head

Join a sunset kayaking trip and keep a look out for seals and dolphins. The drive from Fethard-on-Sea to Hook Head passes ruined castles, secluded bays and a lighthouse.

🕑 ½ day

River Barrow

Wexford ●
Wexford Harbour

Rosslare Point

Saltee Islands

Take a ferry to the uninhabited Saltee Islands to see seals and spot puffins and other seabirds.

🕑 ½ day

Rosslare ○ Harbour

Tacumshin Lake

Lady's Island Lake

Waterford Harbour

○ Fethard-on-Sea

Ballyteige Bay

○ Chour

Carnsore Point

Baginbun Head

Forlorn Point

Hook Peninsula

Hook Head

Saltee Islands

St George's Channel

WILD WEST COAST
Trip Builder

TAKE YOUR PICK OF MUST-SEES AND HIDDEN GEMS

▬▬ Ireland's northwest offers unspoilt natural beauty: wild and remote headlands where winding coastal paths look out over jagged cliffs, lonely lighthouses and long sandy bays. Gaelic culture thrives in the Irish-speaking regions, where trad music sessions take place most nights.

🗺️ Trip Notes

Hub towns Galway, Sligo

How long Around a week

Getting around Hiring a car is the best option since public transport doesn't serve the most remote areas. Tory Island and Clare Island are reached by ferry.

Tips The Wild Atlantic Way (wildatlanticway.com) coastal driving route traverses Ireland's west coast. The signage is helpful but the route can be congested; if possible avoid the busy summer months.

Tory Island
Walk the island's rugged coastline and spot puffins on the cliffs. Stay on the island overnight to join in the dancing at a trad session.
🕐 *1-2 days*

Atlantic Ocean

Achill Island

Clare Island
Follow in the footsteps of Ireland's pirate queen Grace O'Malley and look for her family motto at Clare Island Abbey. Back on the mainland, climb Croagh Patrick.
🕐 *1 day*

ⓝ 0   40 km
0   20 miles

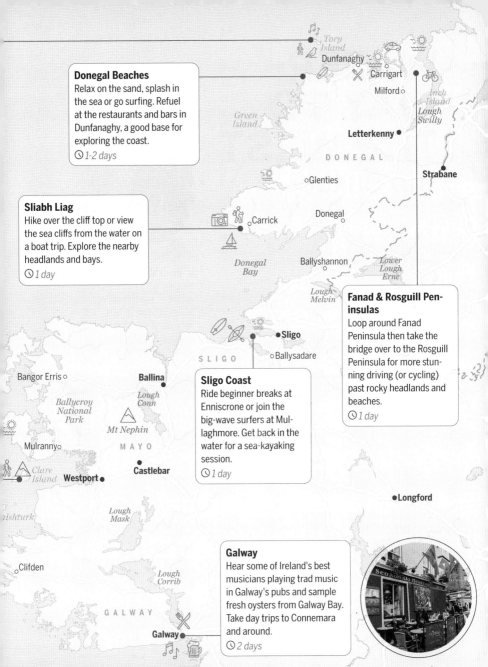

Donegal Beaches
Relax on the sand, splash in the sea or go surfing. Refuel at the restaurants and bars in Dunfanaghy, a good base for exploring the coast.
🕑 1-2 days

Sliabh Liag
Hike over the cliff top or view the sea cliffs from the water on a boat trip. Explore the nearby headlands and bays.
🕑 1 day

Fanad & Rosguill Peninsulas
Loop around Fanad Peninsula then take the bridge over to the Rosguill Peninsula for more stunning driving (or cycling) past rocky headlands and beaches.
🕑 1 day

Sligo Coast
Ride beginner breaks at Enniscrone or join the big-wave surfers at Mullaghmore. Get back in the water for a sea-kayaking session.
🕑 1 day

Galway
Hear some of Ireland's best musicians playing trad music in Galway's pubs and sample fresh oysters from Galway Bay. Take day trips to Connemara and around.
🕑 2 days

Tory Island
Dunfanaghy
Carrigart
Milford
Inch Island
Lough Swilly
Green Island
Letterkenny
DONEGAL
Strabane
Glenties
Donegal
Carrick
Donegal Bay
Ballyshannon
Lower Lough Erne
Lough Melvin
Lough Conn
Sligo
Ballysadare
SLIGO
Bangor Erris
Ballina
Ballycroy National Park
Mt Nephin
MAYO
Mulranny
Clare Island
Westport
Castlebar
Longford
inishturk
Lough Mask
Clifden
Lough Corrib
GALWAY
Galway

WATER-WAY TO THE WEST
Trip Builder

TAKE YOUR PICK OF MUST-SEES AND HIDDEN GEMS

■■■■ The River Shannon waterway offers a peaceful, slow-paced trip through the rolling landscapes of inland Ireland. Where the river meets the Atlantic, the scenery is dramatic: raggedly beautiful Loop Head, the vertical Cliffs of Moher and the mesmerising landscapes of the Burren.

🗺 Trip Notes

Hub towns Carrick-on-Shannon, Limerick

How long Around a week

Getting around Follow the path of the River Shannon by car, bike or boat. Carrick-on-Shannon is a good place to begin boat trips since it has convenient public transport links.

Tips Hire a liveaboard motor cruiser for a holiday on the River Shannon. No licence is required; the boats travel very slowly (most have a maximum speed of 10 to 15 knots).

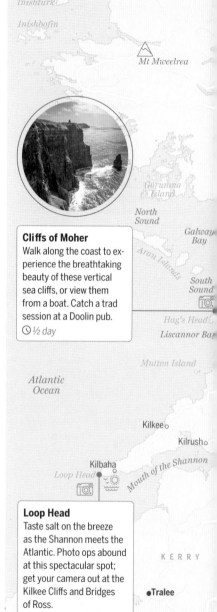

Inishturk

Inishbofin

Mt Mweelrea

Cliffs of Moher
Walk along the coast to experience the breathtaking beauty of these vertical sea cliffs, or view them from a boat. Catch a trad session at a Doolin pub.
🕐 ½ day

Gorumna Island

North Sound

Galway Bay

Aran Islands

South Sound

Hag's Head

Liscannor Bay

Mutton Island

Atlantic Ocean

Kilkee ○

Kilrush ○

Kilbaha

Loop Head ●

Mouth of the Shannon

Loop Head
Taste salt on the breeze as the Shannon meets the Atlantic. Photo ops abound at this spectacular spot; get your camera out at the Kilkee Cliffs and Bridges of Ross.
🕐 1 day

KERRY

● Tralee

ROSCOMMON

Lough Ree
Splash with the family at an inflatable water park and look out for migratory birds, including whooper swans and curlews.
🕐 1 day

Lough Ree

WESTMEATH

● Athlone

Lough Mask

Lough Corrib

Ballinasloe○

GALWAY

Galway ●

Tullamore ●

The Burren
Hike through a remarkable landscape of barren grey limestone in the Burren. The area's ancient sites, wildlife and starkly beautiful scenery can be explored via numerous walking trails.
🕐 1-2 days

Lough Derg
Visit the monastic settlement at Inis Cealtra by boat to see high crosses, a round tower and several churches. History buffs will enjoy the sights of picturesque Killaloe.
🕐 1 day

Black Head

Ballyvaughan

The Burren

○Lisdoonvarna

○Portumna

○Ennistimon

Lough Derg

Nenagh○

Ennis●

CLARE

River Shannon

Shannon Estuary

Labasheeda○

Foynes○

Askeaton

●Limerick

River Dead

○Tarbert

LIMERICK

Foynes
Stop at the village of Foynes to learn about its connection to the first commercial transatlantic passenger flight.
🕐 ½ day

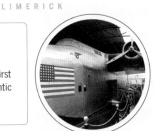

●Tipperary   TIPPERARY

River Tar

🧭 N   0 ____ 40 km
        0 ____ 20 miles

7 Things to Know About
IRELAND

INSIDER TIPS TO HIT THE GROUND RUNNING

1 The Gaeltacht

Gaeltachtaí are regions where Irish (Gaeilge) is the primary spoken language. They include large areas of Counties Donegal, Mayo, Galway and Kerry and parts of Counties Cork, Meath and Waterford. Here you are likely to hear Irish being spoken among locals, although everyone will be able to speak English, too. In the summer, several places in Gaeltachtaí offer Irish language courses for all levels.

2 Making Conversation

Irish people are generally friendly but often reserved, and tend to avoid topics that might cause embarrassment. Don't be too direct too soon, especially if discussing politics, which can be a touchy subject. Humour is the exception: ribbing can get quite personal but it's usually not meant to offend. The Irish sense of humour can be quite dark, and few topics are off limits when it comes to making a joke.

3 Time for Tea

Tea is the unofficial national drink and many Irish people drink several cups a day. Expect to be offered a cuppa upon entering someone's home. Biscuits will be provided for dunking.

4 Eat Early

Restaurants tend to close much earlier than elsewhere in Europe. In rural areas kitchens may shut as early as 8pm; plan ahead.

▶ See more about Irish cuisine on p16

5 Expect Rain

Ireland's climate is generally mild and changeable. Rain is a possibility almost every day of the year – but so is sunshine. Bring a raincoat (umbrellas aren't much help in the wind) and wear layers you can take off when the sun comes out. Sometimes it snows for a few days in winter, but not always.

▶ See more about the seasons on p22

7 Pub Culture

Pubs are where people in Ireland gather to share stories and drink pints. It's usual for friends to take turns to buy a round of drinks for the whole group. Local musicians often gather for informal trad sessions, which usually take place at a pub table.

▶ See more about pints and trad sessions on p18

6 Local Lingo

Banjaxed Broken beyond repair or very drunk.

Bold Naughty; usually used with children ('don't be bold').

Craic Fun. Can be used in a greeting ('what's the craic?'), to describe a good time ('great craic') or for someone fun to hang out with ('she's good craic').

Dander Walk ('let's take a dander to the shops').

Eejit An idiot or fool. Often used affectionately ('you big eejit').

Gas Funny; can be used to describe a person or situation.

Grand Great, good or fine ('you're grand').

Lash Many uses, including to go out drinking ('out on the lash') or for rain ('it's lashing down').

Quare Used for emphasis ('there's a quare wind blowing').

Yoke Any nearby object.

Many Irish people swear a lot so be prepared to hear some colourful language. Curse words can be part of everyday speech and are not necessarily intended to be insulting or cause offence.

▶ See the Language chapter on p250

Read, Listen, Watch & Follow

 READ

Milkman
(Anna Burns; 2018) A darkly funny perspective on life during the Troubles.

Don't Touch My Hair
(Emma Dabiri; 2019) Dabiri uses hair to examine slavery, colonisation and cultural appropriation.

Angela's Ashes
(Frank McCourt; 1996) A bleak story of poverty-stricken childhood in Limerick.

The Sea
(John Banville; 2005) An engrossing meditation on grief and memory, set in Wexford.

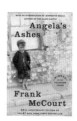

 LISTEN

Go Bravely
(Denise Chaila; 2020) Thought-provoking hip-hop by a Zambian-Irish rapper, poet and singer.

First Prize Bravery
(Sorcha Richardson; 2019) Poppy, breezy folk music by an up-and-coming singer-songwriter from Dublin.

A Hero's Death
(Fontaines DC; 2020; pictured right) The Dublin post-punk band's follow-up to their hit album Dogrel has the same sense of urgency and rage.

Irish History Podcast
Fin Dwyer's podcast covers everything from the Norman Invasion to the Great Famine.

The Blindboy Podcast
Hosted by Blindboy of comedy hip-hip duo the Rubberbandits, with interviews, short fiction and comedy.

WATCH

Normal People (2020) TV series based on Sally Rooney's 2018 novel, set in Sligo and Dublin.

Derry Girls (2018–present) Derry schoolgirls are the stars of this TV comedy set in the 1990s.

Wolfwalkers (2020) The third animation in Kilkenny-based Cartoon Saloon's Irish folklore trilogy.

Good Vibrations (2013) The story of record-label owner Terri Hooley and Belfast's punk rock scene.

Michael Collins (1996) Liam Neeson stars in Neil Jordan's Oscar-winning biopic.

TOP: © 2020 WOLFWALKERS. WOLFWALKERS IS A REGISTERED TRADEMARK OF CARTOON SALOON/MELUSINE. ALL RIGHTS RESERVED. BOTTOM: GETTY IMAGES/HANDOUT ©

FOLLOW

The Taste
(thetaste.ie)
Food, drink and travel, including reviews.

@Ireland
Curated by a new person each week on Twitter.

Life of Stuff

The Life of Stuff
(thelifeofstuff. com) Irish travel, culture and lifestyle blog.

@DiscoverIreland
Photos and tourism news on Twitter.

@Chrishillphotographer
Inspiring Instagram account.

Sate your Ireland dreaming with a virtual vacation

DUBLIN

CULTURE | HISTORY | COAST

Experience
Dublin
online

Bonus Online Experiences

▶ **The Sound of Dublin**

▶ **Dublin Spectres and Spirits**

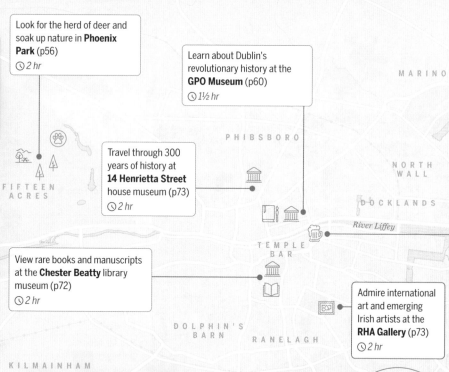

Look for the herd of deer and soak up nature in **Phoenix Park** (p56)
🕐 *2 hr*

Learn about Dublin's revolutionary history at the **GPO Museum** (p60)
🕐 *1½ hr*

MARINO

PHIBSBORO

NORTH WALL

Travel through 300 years of history at **14 Henrietta Street** house museum (p73)
🕐 *2 hr*

FIFTEEN ACRES

DOCKLANDS

River Liffey

TEMPLE BAR

View rare books and manuscripts at the **Chester Beatty** library museum (p72)
🕐 *2 hr*

DOLPHIN'S BARN

RANELAGH

Admire international art and emerging Irish artists at the **RHA Gallery** (p73)
🕐 *2 hr*

KILMAINHAM

DUBLIN
Trip Builder

▬▬▬ Explore the city on foot, dipping into museums, galleries, old pubs or live performances, or pack a picnic and take a day trip out of the city for some coastal walks and sea air, perhaps spotting some wildlife along the way.

Explore bookable experiences in Dublin online

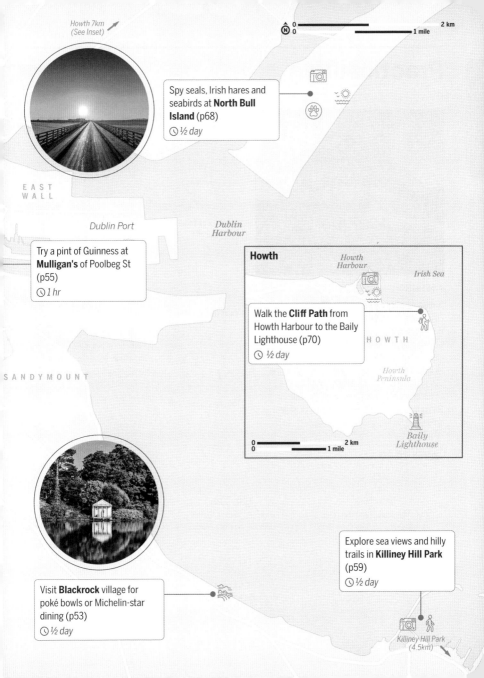

Spy seals, Irish hares and seabirds at **North Bull Island** (p68)
🕐 ½ day

Howth 7km (See Inset) ↗

Try a pint of Guinness at **Mulligan's** of Poolbeg St (p55)
🕐 1 hr

EAST WALL

Dublin Port

Dublin Harbour

SANDYMOUNT

Howth

Howth Harbour

Irish Sea

Walk the **Cliff Path** from Howth Harbour to the Baily Lighthouse (p70)
🕐 ½ day

H O W T H

Howth Peninsula

Baily Lighthouse

| 0 | 2 km |
| 0 | 1 mile |

Explore sea views and hilly trails in **Killiney Hill Park** (p59)
🕐 ½ day

Visit **Blackrock** village for poké bowls or Michelin-star dining (p53)
🕐 ½ day

Killiney Hill Park (4.5km) ↘

N

| 0 | 2 km |
| 0 | 1 mile |

Practicalities

ABD/SHUTTERSTOCK ©

ARRIVING

Dublin Airport The Airlink Express bus to Dublin city centre costs €6 online (dublinbus.ie) or €7 from the airport. Aircoach buses to the city cost €8 and also run to various suburbs. Taxis to the city centre cost from €25 to €40.
Heuston & Connolly Stations Trains from the south and west of Ireland arrive into Heuston, which connects to bus routes and the Luas tram. Trains from the north and southeast of Ireland arrive into Connolly, which also connects to the DART and Luas.

HOW MUCH FOR A

Cup of tea
€2.90

Pint of Guinness
€5.50

Toasted sandwich
€7

GETTING AROUND

Walk The city is very easy to navigate on foot.

Bus Dublin Bus operates the county-wide network. Buses run from around 6am to 11.30pm with late-night options at weekends. Download the Dublin Bus app for live timetables.

Rail There are two Luas tram lines to the suburbs, and the DART train runs along the coast northbound to Howth or Malahide and southbound to Greystones. A Leap Card (deposit €5) gives discounted fares on bus, Luas, DART and rail; 1-day, 3-day or 7-day Leap Visitor Cards give unlimited journeys.

WHEN TO GO

JAN - MAR
Chilly temperatures and short days; evenings brighter towards March.

APR - JUN
Warmer temperatures and drier days, but pack for showers.

JUL - SEP
Warmest (Jul–Aug) and driest weather, but always changeable.

OCT - DEC
Temperatures much cooler, with shorter days and darker evenings.

EATING & DRINKING

Fish and chips For a traditional takeaway, try smoked cod and chips from Leo Burdock in Christchurch and Temple Bar, or Beshoffs on O'Connell St, or dine in and pair beer-battered fish and chips with natural wine at Fish Shop on Benburb St.

Irish breakfast Sausages, bacon, black and white puddings, tomato, eggs, toast and a pot of tea – if the 'full Irish' isn't available at your accommodation, be sure to try it at a cafe.

Must-try sandwich
The Sunday roast
sandwich at Tír Deli (P54)

Best seafood truck
Salty Buoy (P54)

CONNECT & FIND YOUR WAY

Wi-fi Most cafes and hotels have free wi-fi and wi-fi is also free on Dublin Bus and Irish Rail.

Navigation The city is divided into postal districts by address – Dublin 2, Dublin 7 – with (mostly) even numbers on the Southside and odd numbers on the Northside.

FOR FREE

Many museums and galleries in Dublin are free, including the three National Museums, the National Gallery, the Chester Beatty, Hugh Lane Gallery and Irish Museum of Modern Art.

WHERE TO STAY

Dublin can be expensive during festivals or big events. Book in advance for the best prices.

Neighbourhood	Pro/Con
St Stephen's Green and Harcourt St	Easy access to museums and galleries of the Georgian area. Nightlife and shopping around Grafton St.
Temple Bar	Right in the action for nightlife and sightseeing. Can be noisy, especially at weekends.
Ballsbridge	Upmarket suburb with good choice of hotels. Around a 20-minute walk to the city centre.
Smithfield	Within walking distance of the city centre and Phoenix Park.
O'Connell St and City Centre	Good mix of hotels plus budget hostels and B&Bs. Stick to main, well-lit areas.
The Liberties	Vibrant area, one of Dublin's oldest. Within walking distance of the city centre.

MONEY

Credit and debit cards are accepted in most retail outlets and there are plenty of ATMs. Don't carry large amounts of cash. Look out for early-bird meal offers, family tickets at attractions and student or senior discounts on tickets.

01 Fair City of Food & STOUT

FOOD | DRINK | HISTORY

Farm-to-fork and seasonal are some of the buzzwords of Dublin's food scene, taking full advantage of Ireland's outstanding produce. Some of the best restaurants are in the suburbs and there's still country pubs within Dublin's borders.

🔍 How to

Getting around For timetables and route planning, download apps from dublinbus.ie and irishrail.ie. The DART train ride along the coast to Blackrock is particularly lovey.

When to go Anytime is a good time to eat, drink and be merry in Dublin – be prepared for crowds and queues during summer.

Money Make sure you have cash on hand, especially for markets and when card machines occasionally go down.

Award-winning It's worth the journey to Blackrock on Dublin's south coast to experience Michelin-quality restaurants like one-Michelin-starred **Liath** (liathrestaurant.com) and Italian restaurant **Volpe Nera** (volpenera.ie), which has a Bib Gourmand.

Strictly seasonal, **Craft** (craftrestaurant.ie) in Harold's Cross serves high-end modern Irish food at very reasonable prices while **Locks Brasserie** (locksrestaurant.ie), which is very popular with locals, serves French cuisine with an Irish twist. There's great views from its location on the Grand Canal.

There are plenty of options for a Middleeast feast like **Brother Hubbard** and **Shakshuka**, but **Shouk** (shouk.ie) in Drumcondra is a Dublin favourite. Their *arayes* (pitas stuffed with spices, onions and lamb or beef) are the best in town.

Weekend Suburban Markets

Hook't Fish&Chips in **Blackrock Market** (theblackrockmarket.com) pride themselves on fresh, locally caught fish and their chips are made the traditional way: hand cut with real Irish spuds. Try smoked meats from Man Street Kitchen at the **Red Stables Market** (@RedStablesMarket) in Raheny on the Northside.

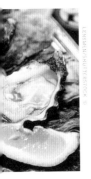

Left Oyster platter **Above left** Temple Bar district **Above right** Olives for sale at a Dublin market stall

Mobile dining The street-food scene has really taken off with a proliferation of amazing food trucks all over Dublin. The competition is fierce, driving up variety and quality.

With tacos to rival the neighbourhood trucks in New York, **La Cocina Cuevas** (lacocinacuevas.com) is worth driving all the way to the far north of County Dublin for. Served alongside Birria Quesa Tacos (slow-cooked beef and Jack cheese), you can practically drink a cup of its Birria consommé,
it's so delicious.

You don't need to hit the coast to salivate over seafood. **The Salty Buoy** (saltybuoy.ie) truck at Peggy Kelly's pub in Harold's Cross is the perfect spot for fresh oysters paired with a pint of Guinness.

Asian street food doesn't get any better than **Bites by Kwanghi** (@bites_by_kwanghi), parked at the **Leopardstown Inn**. It's difficult to pick between the hoisin pulled pork and Korean fried chicken, so just have both.

✕ Sandwich Obsession

Irish people love sandwiches. Dublin's food scene may be incredibly diverse, but a classic toastie is still an obsession – especially washed down with a creamy pint, which **Grogan's** (groganspub.ie) in the city centre are the champions of.

Malahide's **Griolladh** (griolladh.ie), which means 'grilling' in Irish, is taking grilled cheese to new heights, perfecting the 'cheese pull' with a triple-cheese blend. Meanwhile, **Tír Deli** (tirfood.ie) in south Dublin specialises in smoked Irish meats. Pair those meats with roasted Irish veg, all tucked into pillowy slices of bread, and you've got yourself a Sunday roast in a sandwich.

John Kavanagh's
CABRA
MARINO
Red Stables Market
Shouk
EAST WALL
Mulligan's
NORTH WALL
Dublin Harbour
Grogan's
Lock's Brasserie
Harold's Cross
Irish Sea
Bites by Kwanghi (2 km)
Blackrock village

0 — 2 km
0 — 1 mile

Left Classic BLT sandwich **Below** John Kavanagh pub, also known as 'The Gravediggers'

Pub life Mulligan's (mulligans.ie) of Poolbeg St has been dubbed 'the home of the pint', serving generations of Dubliners. James Joyce was a regular here. But **Leonard's Corner** (@leonards corner) is a worthy rival in the beer stakes. 'The Leonard' is a neighbourhood gem near the Grand Canal and the barman here prides himself on pulling the best pint in Dublin.

Built into the wall of one of Dublin's oldest cemeteries in the neighbourhood of Glasnevin in north Dublin, **John Kavanagh** has quenched the thirst of gravediggers since 1833 – hence its local name, '**The Gravediggers**' (@gravediggers2). The beautiful Victorian interior has changed very little with no music or television. Perfect for a quiet pint and conversation.

Country vibes Set in the foothills of the Dublin Mountains, **The Blue Light** (thebluelight.ie) is a country bar with the best drinking views in the county. It's a favourite for its regular music sessions, a cosy fireplace and outdoor seating across the road for summer days.

In west Dublin on the north side of the River Liffey, **The Wren's Nest** (thewrensnest.ie) in the Strawberry Beds valley is a true country pub with roots going back to the late 16th century. Guinness was bottled here until the 1960s, so they know a thing or two about 'the black stuff'.

02 Family Fun in **THE PARK**

PARKS | FAMILY | WILDLIFE

Step into a sprawling Dublin green space and be whisked away from the bustle of the metropolis. Spend the day discovering why Dubliners are such fans of the great outdoors with their attractive parks and gardens.

🗺 How to

Getting around
There's no need to hire a car in Dublin city. Well serviced by many transport links, parks are easily accessible for solo adventurers or family days out.

When to go Parks are busiest when there's a bit of heat during May to August and whenever the sun is out.

Picnics Join locals taking their lunchtime breaks in urban spaces like St Stephen's Green and Dubhlinn Gardens.

Oasis of calm The famous **Garden of Remembrance** on O'Connell St is much loved as a beautiful resting place, despite being right in the centre of the metropolis. It's dedicated to 'all those who gave their lives in the cause of Irish Freedom'.

One of the city's most unusual parks is **Blessington Street Basin**, also known as Dublin's 'Secret Garden'. It's less than 15 minutes' walk north from O'Connell St and about 80% of it is water. Surrounded by high stone walls, the park was formerly the city reservoir but is now a peaceful retreat for locals.

A slice of urban wild Roaming free, the wild deer in **Phoenix Park** were first introduced in the 1600s. This impressive open space just 3km west of the centre is the largest enclosed city park in Europe. Locally known as 'The Phoeno', it has 707 hectares of recreational

⚘ Become a Tree Detective

Kids can learn all about Ireland's native species in selected parks by downloading Nature Tree Trail packs (dublincity.ie). The activity packs include family-friendly discovery routes as well as facts about the trees found across the city's parks. Bring a pencil and paper for rubbings.

Left Garden of Remembrance
Above left Fallow deer, Phoenix Park
Above right Tulips, National Botanic Gardens (p58)

space to explore and it's an important site of urban biodiversity. Nearby **Dublin Zoo** is also a family favourite.

The **National Botanic Gardens** in Glasnevin is a heavenly, peaceful place for a stroll – particularly on a summer's day. Visitors of all ages will be enthralled by its extensive grounds, walled gardens and restored glasshouses. Right next door is **Glasnevin Cemetery**, another historical landmark that is accessible via a walkway from the Botanic Gardens. Perfect for a stroll on an autumn afternoon.

Beyond Dublin Centre

Hotfoot it to **St Anne's Park** (Clontarf East) for acres of green space just 30 minutes from the centre by Dublin Bus. The park is top for dog owners, with a space specifically for dogs to meet up and make friends.

👪 Places for Parents

Corkagh Park Often overlooked, this Clondalkin park is a green jewel in an expanding city. The 120 hectares has rolling hills, native trees, a rose garden, a fairy wood, a Viking-themed playground, fishing lakes and even its own campsite.

St Stephen's Green Complete with a playground for tots and enough signs of the city's living history for older kids, the Green's location is ideal for a quick breather between shopping and snacking.

Marlay Park This park in the Southside suburbs of Rathfarnham and Ballinteer has cafes, craft shops, playgrounds, sports facilities and even a miniature railway.

Recommended by Peter Kavanagh, podcaster and Clondalkin politician @thekavofficial

Left St Stephen's Green **Below** Mute swan, Blackrock Park

On Saturday mornings, see people practicing tai chi organised by Suaimhneas (taichi chuan.ie) in front of the entrance to the walled garden. St Anne's also has a Remote-Control Car Track, where racers take their miniature cars out on the tracks while onlookers cheer from the sidelines.

Parks outside Dublin's urban core are usually quieter. With views of Dublin Bay, **Blackrock Park** is 30 minutes southbound from the centre and has a pleasant cycle path, outdoor exercise equipment and a serene pond complete with an island.

Further south, do as the locals do and take a hike in **Killiney Hill Park**. Enjoy incredible views and ships across the Irish Sea and gaze towards Dalkey Island. The pathways here are brushed by woodland and vibrant yellow gorse. The park is accessible as a day trip from the city centre and is a 20-minute walk from the DART station at Killiney.

Heading 30 minutes northwest from central Dublin, **Tolka Valley Regional Park** is another worthy escape, with undulating fields, tranquil meadowlands and a babbling river slicing through 300 acres.

03 Revolutionary **DUBLIN**

HISTORY | CULTURE | LANDMARKS

▬▬▬ Dublin is where many of Ireland's most subversive moments took place during the 1900s. The country went through many turbulent revolts to separate itself from British rule in the early part of the 20th century, most notably three revolutionary conflicts – the 1916 Easter Rising, the War of Independence and the Irish Civil War.

SEAMICK PHOTO/SHUTTERSTOCK ©

🗺 How to

Getting around City centre revolutionary sites are easily accessed by foot. For places further away like Glasnevin Cemetery, take the local Dublin Bus or cycle using the bike-share scheme (dublinbikes.ie).

When to go Top attractions are particularly popular with tourists come summertime.

Hear the Proclamation Commemoration of the 1916 Rising takes place on Easter Sunday morning outside the GPO. The National Flag is lowered at noon and the Proclamation is read.

DAMIEN STORAN/SHUTTERSTOCK ©

PETER KROCKA/SHUTTERSTOCK ©

Left Glasnevin Cemetery **Far left top** Four Courts **Far left bottom** Reading of the Proclamation

DUBLIN EXPERIENCES

Whirlwind Tour

A taste of revolution Dublin's impressive General Post Office, opened in 1818, houses the **GPO Museum** commemorating the 1916 Easter Rising. The GPO itself is a landmark of great significance to modern Irish history, as the former headquarters of the uprising leaders. It was from outside here that Patrick Pearse read out the Proclamation of the Irish Republic.

Within walking distance of the GPO, **The Four Courts** (Inns Quay) is where the Civil War began on 28 June 1922, when the National Army attacked an anti-Treaty garrison. The fighting raged for 60 hours.

Iconic women Though women played a vital part in the revolution, there are few landmarks that represent their input. Two notable exceptions are the statue of nationalist Constance Markievicz with her beloved dog Poppett on Tara St and, further afield in Fingal, a plaque to Mary 'Molly' Adrian on the bridge in the charming village of Oldtown. Molly was a veteran of the 1916 Rising and the director of the Lusk branch of Cumann na mBan, an all-female auxiliary group.

Echoes of conflict During the early 20th century right through to 1923, many revolutionaries fell. Some of the most important leaders and suffragists are commemorated at **Glasnevin Cemetery**. Here you can find the graves of fighters including humanitarian Roger Casement, writer Arthur Griffith and suffragette Maud Gonne. **Arbour Hill Cemetery** is the burial place of 14 leaders of the Rising including Patrick Pearse and James Connolly, who were executed at Kilmainham Gaol in 1916.

Revolutionary Women

Despite the lack of physical Dublin tributes, the importance of Irish women during the conflicts cannot go unmentioned.

Cumann na mBan, an all-female auxiliary who partook in the fight for Irish freedom, was founded at **Wynn's Hotel** in 1914.

Nearby, **44 Gardiner St** has a memorial plaque honouring Molly O'Reilly. As a teenager, she raised the symbolic green flag with the gold harp over Liberty Hall before the 1916 Rising.

During the Civil War, many women were imprisoned at **Kilmainham Gaol**, including political cartoonist Grace Gifford Plunkett whose restored mural can still be seen there.

Recommended by tour guide Marteen Lane (marteenlane.com; @marteenlane)

KEY PLAYERS
in a Revolution

01 Thomas J Clarke
A leading figure in the Irish Republican Brotherhood (IRB). The first signatory of the Proclamation of the Irish Republic.

02 Patrick Pearse
Irish language activist and headmaster, Pearse was the military and political leader of the rebel forces in the Easter Rising (1916).

03 Francis Sheehy-Skeffington
Dedicated pacifist and suffragist, murdered by a British military officer during the Rising after being taken hostage.

04 Joseph Plunkett
Born into a wealthy family, Plunkett was the main military strategist for the rebel military forces during the Rising.

05 Roger Casement
Humanitarian and 1916 leader who exposed abuses in the Congo. He was convicted of high treason against the Crown and hanged in London.

06 Constance Markievicz
Suffragette and nationalist, she was elected Minister for Labour in the First Dáil. The first female cabinet minister in Europe.

07 Kathleen Lynn
The chief medical officer with the Irish Citizen Army during the Rising. She was imprisoned in Kilmainham Gaol with Markievicz.

08 Elizabeth O'Farrell
Arguably part of the most pivotal moment of the Rising by delivering the message of surrender to the British troops.

09 Grace Gifford Plunkett
A political cartoonist who married Joseph Plunkett hours before his execution. Following the Rising, she produced much nationalist propaganda.

10 Michael Collins
Played a leading role throughout the Irish struggle for independence. He was director of intelligence for the IRA and leader of the IRB.

11 Arthur Griffith
Founder of the party Sinn Féin, Griffith led the Irish negotiations that produced the Anglo-Irish Treaty. Signed it with Collins.

12 Éamon de Valera
Fought in the Rising, became the political leader of the Irish revolutionary movement. Later was Taoiseach and President of Ireland.

13 Maud Gonne
Suffragette and republican revolutionary who opposed the Treaty. She set up the Womens' Prisoner Defence League.

A Nation Divided

HOW IRELAND BECAME TWO STATES

The Irish Revolution encompassed a series of events that marked incredible political upheaval across the island. Understanding the impact of the country's most turbulent times makes a visit to Ireland and its capital city Dublin a more enriching experience.

By 1912, Irish nationalism was on the rise and Irish Home Rule legislation was due to be passed by the British parliament in Westminster. Home Rule would give Ireland limited self-government within the British Empire. Irish unionists – those who wished to remain under British rule, mainly based in northeast Ulster – intended to resist Home Rule, primarily in the form of a militia known as the Ulster Volunteer Force (UVF).

In response, the nationalist Irish Volunteers were formed as a defensive militia. However, a separatist minority in Ireland, represented by the secret society known as the Irish Republican Brotherhood (IRB), desired complete Irish independence and an end to 700 years of British rule.

As Irish historian Gerard Shannon explains, 'Key leaders of the IRB infiltrated the Volunteers to use the organisation as a means for rebellion. Their chance came with the outbreak of WWI in 1914. With thousands of Irishmen joining the British army and dying in the trenches of Europe, the IRB believed "England's difficulty was Ireland's opportunity".' Their planned insurrection, the Easter Rising, took place in April 1916. A Proclamation signed by the leaders declared the independent Irish Republic and over 1500 rebels took over key locations in Dublin. However, the British military crushed them after a week and the leading figures were executed.

Aftermath of the Rising

Gerard notes that following this conflict there was an upsurge of sympathy for the rebels. The separatist party Sinn Féin, wrongly blamed for the Rising, won over 70 seats at the 1918 British general election. With their elec-

Left Proclamation of the Irish Respublic **Middle** Kilmainham Gaol (p75) **Right** Easter Parade commemorating the 1916 Rising

toral mandate, the Sinn Féin MPs formed Dáil Éireann, an Irish parliament for the independent Irish Republic declared in 1916.

From January 1919, the Irish War of Independence began. The Irish Republic's underground institutions acted as a counter-state to the British administration in Ireland. The resurgent Irish Volunteers, now known as the Irish Republican Army (IRA), began a guerrilla campaign and intelligence war against the British forces in Ireland. The war ended with a truce in July 1921, and Sinn Féin representatives negotiated the Anglo-Irish Treaty with the British cabinet that December. This lead to the creation of the Irish Free State – not a republic, but a self-governing dominion of the British Empire. It consisted of 26 counties. The remaining six counties of northeast Ulster made up Northern Ireland, governed by a unionist majority, functioning as its own entity within the United Kingdom.

> With thousands of Irishmen joining the British army and dying in the trenches of Europe, the IRB believed 'England's difficulty was Ireland's opportunity'.

A bitter political split followed in both Sinn Féin and the IRA. Those opposed felt the Free State fell far short of an independent Irish Republic and was a betrayal of what was fought for. Those in support felt the Free State could be used as an eventual 'stepping stone' to complete freedom for Ireland. This dispute led to the Irish Civil War, beginning in June 1922. The intensely violent conflict lasted 11 months and ended in victory for the Irish Free State. In 1948, the Free State declared itself as the independent Republic of Ireland and withdrew from the British Commonwealth.

🎬 Revolutionary Moments on Film

Michael Collins (1996) Though this film by Neil Jordan was criticised for some historical inaccuracies, Liam Neeson was widely praised for his passionate portrayal of the 1916 leader.

Rebellion (2016) This five-part serial drama told the story of the 1916 Rising through the perspective of characters living through the political turbulence.

Mise Éire (1959) Newsreels and original footage feature in this documentary about the revolutionary events in 1916 and following years.

The Wind that Shakes the Barley (2006) An action-packed drama about brothers during the War of Independence. Ken Loach's film won Palme d'Or at the 2006 Cannes Film Festival.

04 Sea Air Around **DALKEY**

SCENIC | COASTAL | ACTIVE

▬▬▬ Pack a picnic and leave the city centre behind for a refreshing coastal walk. This one starts in the heritage town of Dalkey, which had seven castles in the Middle Ages and still has ruins. You can walk up steps through a forest trail to the top of Killiney or Dalkey Hill for beautiful sea views, or take a stroll on the pebble beach.

LAURIE NOBLE/GETTY IMAGES ©

🗺 **How to**

Getting there Take the DART from the city centre to Dalkey station (around 30 minutes, irishrail.ie). If driving, park at Dalkey DART station or use on-street parking (fees apply). There are some steep hills and the walk goes through a park so is not suitable for bikes.

When to go Year-round, but spring, summer and autumn are the nicest times.

Top tip Drop in to **Select Stores** (selectstoresdalkey.ie) in Dalkey for fresh juices and smoothies.

⛵ **Top of the Rock**

Granite was pulled out of **Dalkey Quarry** for many years — the covetable rock was used to build Dún Laoghaire Piers from 1815 to 1817, as well as the Great South Wall at Dublin Port in 1795. Nowadays the disused quarry is a popular rock-climbing location. Organise lessons with Go Beyond Adventure (gobeyond adventure.ie).

Bullock Harbour

05 At Bullock Harbour visit the ruins of **Bullock Castle**, which dates from 1205, or take a kayaking tour along the coast back to Dalkey Island (kayaking.ie).

Harbour Rd

Ulverton Rd

01 Visit **Dalkey Castle and Heritage Centre** (pictured left) for a one-hour tour that includes a live theatre performance, exhibitions on local heritage and a writer's gallery.

Coliemore Harbour

Castle St

Coliemore Rd

Sorrento Rd

Dalkey Island

04 Coliemore Harbour is a hub for fishing and diving. Take the small ferry across to **Dalkey Island** (summer months) or visit nearby Biddy's Cottage (86 Coliemore Rd) for food and storytelling.

Dalkey Ave

Killiney Hill Park

Vico Rd

02 **Killiney Hill Park** has looped trails to the top of Dalkey Hill and Killiney Hill, as well as superb views over Dublin Bay, Killiney Bay and to the Sugarloaf Mountain.

03 Walk the **Vico Road** back to the village to enjoy more sea views – there are steps down to White Rock bathing place, which connects to Killiney Beach at low tide.

Irish Sea

MARC DUFRESNE/GETTY IMAGES ©,
IRENE FOX/SHUTTERSTOCK ©,
LUKAS PENDEK/SHUTTERSTOCK ©

N

0   500 m
0   0.25 miles

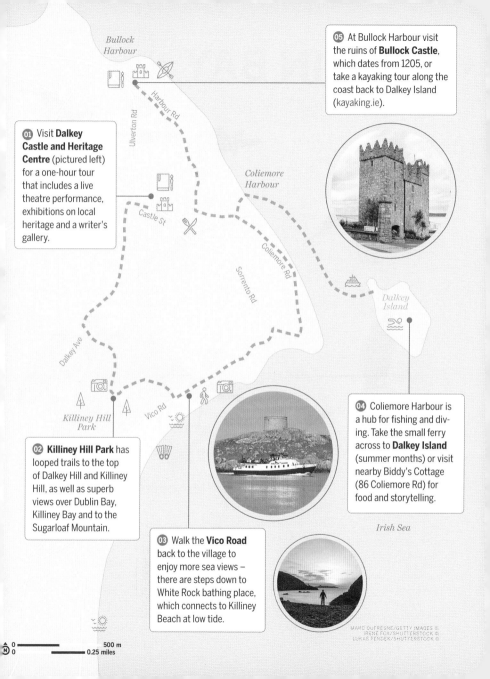

DUBLIN BAY
Wildlife

01 Gulls
Gulls are present year-round, including Mediterranean gulls, black-headed gulls and herring gulls, which nest around Dalkey Island.

02 Cormorants
These birds are often spotted sitting on rocks around the bay, spreading out their wings to dry after diving for fish.

03 Terns
Some of Europe's rarest seabirds, Arctic terns, sandwich terns, common terns and roseate terns are all regular visitors to the bay.

04 Oystercatchers
Easy to spot with their bright orange bills and pink legs, oystercatchers wade around rocky areas looking for worms and shellfish to feed on.

05 Brent geese
Light-bellied brent geese migrate from Arctic Canada for autumn and winter – they are spotted around North Bull Island and Booterstown Nature Reserve.

06 Grey herons
Lone grey herons are often spotted sitting motionless on rocks along the shore around the bay, ready to strike for prey.

07 Short-eared owls
Often found hunting, seen most often on North Bull Island and sometimes on Dalkey Island.

08 Seals
There are populations of both common seals and larger grey seals at North Bull Island and at Lamb Island beside Dalkey Island.

09 Porpoises and dolphins
Harbour porpoises are often spotted around Dalkey Island, while small pods of bottlenose and common dolphins can be found in the bay.

10 Rabbits and hares
There are Irish hares and rabbits in the grasslands at North Bull Island, and Dalkey Island also has a population of rabbits.

11 Butterflies
Species that favour Dublin Bay include the marsh fritillary butterfly, with its orange and cream-patterned wings.

12 Jellyfish
These include common jellyfish, transparent with four distinct rings, which are often spotted drifting around the bay between April and September.

05
Hiking in
HOWTH

ACTIVE | SEAFOOD | OUTDOORS

Long ago Howth was an island, and to this day there's still something about the place that gives it an island vibe. Take a walk on the cliffs or hike through the gorse on Howth Head to shake off the big city and work up an appetite for fresh seafood in the village.

How to

Getting here The best way to get to Howth from Dublin city is by DART (around 26 minutes) or Dublin Bus (number 31).

When to go Spring and summer for fragrant gorse and rhododendrons. The harbour and main Cliff Path can get crowded on sunny weekends and holidays.

Tasty tip Howth is a fishing village, so this is the place to tuck into fish and chips; the freshest are from **Beshoffs** (beshoffs.ie).

The Insider Scoop on Howth

Sign up for a four-hour **Howth Safari Hiking Tour** with Shane's Howth Adventures (shane showthadventures. com) to learn all about the nature and history of the Howth peninsula. Shane will take you to Howth Castle and the Cliff Path, sharing local legends and references while pointing out secret trails along the way.

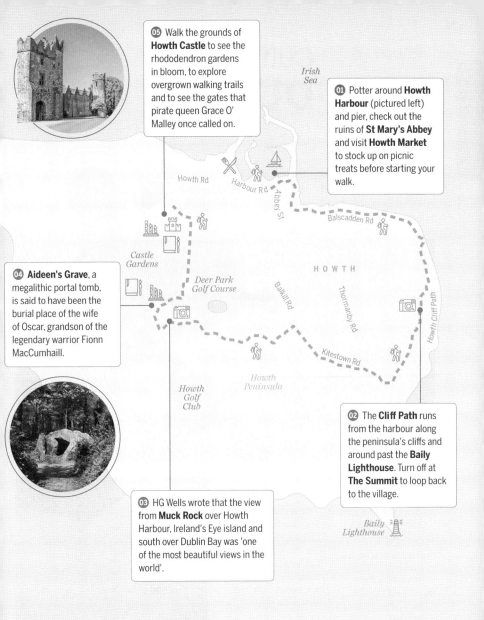

05 Walk the grounds of **Howth Castle** to see the rhododendron gardens in bloom, to explore overgrown walking trails and to see the gates that pirate queen Grace O' Malley once called on.

01 Potter around **Howth Harbour** (pictured left) and pier, check out the ruins of **St Mary's Abbey** and visit **Howth Market** to stock up on picnic treats before starting your walk.

Irish Sea

Howth Rd

Harbour Rd

Abbey St

Balscadden Rd

Castle Gardens

HOWTH

Deer Park Golf Course

Balkill Rd

Thormanby Rd

Howth Cliff Path

04 Aideen's Grave, a megalithic portal tomb, is said to have been the burial place of the wife of Oscar, grandson of the legendary warrior Fionn MacCumhaill.

Kitestown Rd

Howth Peninsula

Howth Golf Club

02 The **Cliff Path** runs from the harbour along the peninsula's cliffs and around past the **Baily Lighthouse**. Turn off at **The Summit** to loop back to the village.

03 HG Wells wrote that the view from **Muck Rock** over Howth Harbour, Ireland's Eye island and south over Dublin Bay was 'one of the most beautiful views in the world'.

Baily Lighthouse

Irish Sea

0
0
1 km
0.5 miles

06 Cultural
DUBLIN

CULTURE | ART | FESTIVALS

One of the best things about Dublin is that you can immerse yourself in culture of all types. One day you can be admiring the Book of Kells, listening to literary stories at the Dublin Writers Museum or learning about 19th-century Irish emigration. The next you might be captivated by some theatre or live music, or swept up in a local festival.

📖 How to

Getting here Most of the main cultural venues are in Dublin city, which is very walkable.

How much Most galleries and museums – such as the National Gallery, the National Museum of Ireland and the RHA – are free. Charges vary for theatre, concerts and live music performances.

Book worms The **Chester Beatty** museum and library in Dublin Castle has a fascinating collection of rare books and manuscripts from around the world.

Left Gandini Juggling, Dublin Dance Festival preview **Far left top** MACNAS arts production, Dublin Fringe Festival **Far left bottom** Koran, Chester Beatty Library

RHA Gallery Has a mix of Irish and international art, with five different galleries, one dedicated to emerging Irish artists. 'I love going to the RHA, it is so immense,' says Sheena Barrett, curator of the LAB Gallery. 'You can see so much work, or see one show if you have a short amount of time.'

National Museum of Ireland – Decorative Arts and History Located in the former Collins Barracks. 'I love when you walk into the square, there is such an incredible feeling of being part of history,' says Sheena. 'I love seeing the Irish designers like Sybil Connolly and I love social history, getting a sense of what people's lives were like, such as when you go into the exhibition of Georgian Dublin and see the extravagant tableware they had.'

14 Henrietta Street Tells the story of how one address went from Georgian townhouse to a tenement dwelling over the years, and the personal stories of those who lived there. 'It's one house seen through the lens of different ages and timeframes,' says Sheena. 'You can physically see the layers of history in the building. The guides are often local Dubs who are passing on memories that their grandparents told them about living in the area.'

EPIC At the fully digital Irish Emigration Museum, you can learn the stories of famous Irish emigrants and about Ireland's impact on the world with everything from music and sport to design and innovation, through interactive exhibits. Afterwards you can explore your own Irish roots at the Irish Family History Centre.

 Best Festivals

Dublin Fringe Festival
Dublin comes alive over 16 days and nights every September with a variety of talent across a range of performing arts. (fringefest.com)

Dublin Dance Festival
Two weeks of the most creative and visionary Irish and international dance performances around the city every May. (dublindancefestival.ie)

International Literature Festival Dublin A two-week May celebration of Irish and international authors, poets, play-wrights, screenwriters and lyricists. Expect readings, guided walks and screen-ings. (ilfdublin.com)

Bloomsday Celebrating the fictional day from James Joyce's *Ulysses*, and its central character Leopold Bloom, with readings and performanc-es every 16 June. (bloomsdayfestival.ie)

Listings

Cosy Pub Snugs

Doheny & Nesbitt

Take your pick of snugs in this Lower Baggot St spot – in Victorian times, these tiny rooms were partitioned off near the bar, for privacy for those who didn't want to be seen.

Toners

You're very lucky if you get a coveted spot in the front snug in Toners, also on Lower Baggot St. It's full of character and poet WB Yeats apparently once drank here.

Kehoes

This South Anne St gem dates to 1803 and you can still see the old wooden partitions, drawers and grocery counter from Victorian times. There's a serving hatch connecting the snug to the bar.

The Stag's Head

There's plenty of room in the snug behind this beautiful Victorian bar in the city. Wood panelling, mirrors, stained-glass windows, plush seats and candlelight add to the atmosphere.

Tea & Cake

Bewley's €

If you like people-watching and buzz, get a pot of Irish breakfast tea and a cherry bun and settle in to soak up the atmosphere in this traditional Grafton Stet cafe.

Queen of Tarts €

Tuck into cakes, seasonal crumbles, delicate pastries and of course delicious tarts of all flavours. There's a branch on Dame St and another nearby on Cow's Lane.

The Shelbourne €€€

Treat yourself to traditional afternoon tea in the Lord Mayor's Lounge overlooking St Stephen's Green, with the full works – tea in china cups and tiered stands with delicate sandwiches, scones and desserts.

Bread 41 €

Grab a seat at the communal table in this Pearse St bakery and tuck into all things sourdough, leaving room for croissants and fresh pastries (arrive early at weekends as things often sell out).

Wall & Keogh €

This Portobello favourite has all types of black, green, yellow and white loose-leaf tea, with everything from Earl Grey and Rooibos to Oolong and Maté, plus a menu of snacks and treats.

 Interactive Exhibits

MoLI

Visit the Museum of Literature Ireland to see the first copy of *Ulysses*, listen to audio advice from Irish writers, and then write the first line of your own novel on a blank page.

Queen of Tarts

CKTRAVELS.COM/SHUTTERSTOCK ©

EPIC

In this fully digital Irish Emigration Museum in Custom House Quay, you can swipe through pages of books, hear stories of Irish characters, send a digital postcard and then explore your Irish roots.

The Little Museum of Dublin

Play a music box, pull the handle on a vintage slot machine and either guide yourself or take a tour around this lovely museum overlooking St Stephen's Green.

Guinness Storehouse

Learn to pull the perfect pint at the Guinness Academy or even put your own face on a pint, before enjoying the views from the rooftop Gravity Bar.

Kilmainham Gaol

Get an idea what it was like to be incarcerated here by standing inside a cell in this jail. It opened in 1796 and various leaders of Irish rebellions have been imprisoned here over the years.

Words on the Street

Marsh's Library

Walk the aisles and soak up the history of Dublin's first library, which opened behind St Patrick's Cathedral in 1707 and has tall bookcases full of old books from all over the world.

Ulysses Rare Books

Browse in this Duke St shop to find your own copies of Irish writers like Patrick Kavanagh, Seamus Heaney and John Banville, plus rare editions of James Joyce, Oscar Wilde and WB Yeats.

Gutter Bookshop

This Temple Bar favourite is the ideal place to stock up on books about Irish history, Irish folk tales and great contemporary Irish writing.

Long Room, Trinity College

SALVADOR MANIQUIZ/SHUTTERSTOCK ©

The Last Bookshop

Drop in to this Camden St treasure trove for books on art, history and literature, with collectibles like Seamus Heaney poetry. Look out for the resident dogs, Bertie and Gussie, too.

Long Room, Trinity

Come here to see the Book of Kells, and soak up the scents from ancient leather bound books – there are more than 200,000 on the shelves and it's been a library since 1732.

Dublin Literary Pub Crawl

Take a fun evening jaunt around some historic Dublin pubs, with live sketches to bring alive the stories of the pubs and the writers associated with them.

Green Escapes

St Stephen's Green

Escape here from the bustle of nearby Grafton St – there's an ornamental lake full of ducks, tree-lined paths and plenty of benches and grassy spots for picnics in good weather.

Iveagh Gardens

Opposite St Stephen's and a bit more rustic than the other parks in the south city. Stroll these gardens to find secret pathways through old trees, a maze, an ancient sundial.

Grand Canal

Take a peaceful walk along the tree-lined banks here, beloved by poet Patrick Kavanagh, and you might spot some wildlife or the resident swans around Portobello.

 ## Spirit of the City

Roe & Co Distillery

Taste the different whiskey ingredients and learn all about distilling on James's St, before shaking up your own cocktail at the Cocktail Workshop Experience and then relaxing in the Power House Bar.

The Dublin Liberties Distillery

Sample a honeycomb liqueur and hear stories of Dublin's medieval days in this working distillery in the Liberties area.

Teeling Whiskey Distillery

Learn how Dublin was once at the centre of the world's whiskey-making, and tour through the production area, copper stills and cask room before a whiskey tasting.

Pearse Lyons Distillery

Look around the old graveyard here, where everyone from sailors to vicars were buried, before exploring the old St James' Church where the working distillery is located.

Jameson Distillery

Tour the original Dublin whiskey experience on Bow St to find out more about how the amber liquid is made, then test the flavours against other whiskeys at a tasting.

 ## Vintage & Antique

Jenny Vander

Browse this Drury St treasure trove for pieces that date as far back as the 1700s, with lots of beaded handbags, scarves and designer jewels from the 19th and early 20th centuries.

Delphi Antiques

Set in a lovely walkway in Powerscourt Townhouse Centre. Dazzle your eyes with an abundance of silver and all types of vintage jewels.

Spindizzy Records

Pop in to the Market Arcade off South Great Georges St to hear vintage sounds and browse vinyl and CDs in all genres. Second-hand dance 12-inches are a speciality.

O'Sullivan Antiques

Francis St in the Liberties is the place for antique furniture – step back in time in this shop for Georgian and Regency pieces, art, statues and lighting.

Nine Crows Vintage

Visit this Temple Bar favourite for a blast from the not-too-distant past with thrift and vintage clothing, including many unworn or on-trend items that have been reworked.

 ## For Foot-Tapping

The Cobblestone

Tap your feet at this Smithfield favourite any night of the week at a traditional music session – there are regular uilleann pipes sessions, plus *sean-nós* ('old-style' songs), *céilidh* (dances) and set dancing.

O'Donoghue's

The famous music bar on Merrion Row where the Dubliners first started. Grab a stool near the front if you want to sing along with one of the regular traditional music sessions here.

Whelan's

Don't miss this famous live music venue on Wexford St, which regularly hosts visiting and local bands of all genres. There are three different stages and the front bar also hosts regular free gigs.

Vicar Street

Book in to this intimate music and comedy venue on Thomas St with around 1,000 seats, for a mix of live music acts and stand-up performers. Look out for Irish favourites, Foil Arms and Hog.

 City Secrets

Dark Dublin Tour

Hear all about the spooky side of the city on this two-hour walking tour with Alternative Dublin, which tells terrifying stories of grave robbing, torture and serial killers from history.

Pat Liddy's Walking Tours

There's very little that Pat and his guides don't know about Dublin's history, so let them show you around and tell you lots of secrets of the streets.

Fab Food Trails

Eat your way around the city and try local Irish produce on this Dublin walking tour, which includes new trends and visits some gastronomic gems.

City Sightseeing Hop-On Hop-Off Bus

The guides on these hop-on, hop-off buses are so entertaining, you might not want to actually get off. It's a great way to get around the city and to places like Kilmainham Gaol.

Dublin Ulysses Tours

Don't worry if you haven't read the book – immerse yourself in all things Joyce on a walking tour of the places that were mentioned in *Ulysses* the novel, starting in the Palace Bar.

 Food with Views

The Winding Stair €€

Irish cuisine overlooking the River Liffey – for a special night, book the small dining area overlooking the Ha'penny Bridge.

Vicar Street

Sophie's at The Dean €€

Absorb 360-degree views of the city over food and cocktails in this popular rooftop restaurant on Harcourt St.

The Pepper Pot €

Take a perch along the balcony in the Powerscourt Townhouse Centre and watch the world go past below as you tuck into tasty breakfast, lunch, coffee or pastries baked on-site.

Oliveto at Haddington House €€

Indulge in Italian food on the patio or garden in Dún Laoghaire, with views of the pier and over to Sandycove, and just a DART ride from the city centre.

Rooftop Bar at The Marker Hotel €€

On a sunny evening, get settled into the rooftop bar of this docklands hotel for views of the Dublin Bay and Dublin Mountains with sunset cocktails and sharing boards.

Canalboat Restaurant €€€

Get on board for a three-hour dinner cruise along part of the Grand Canal in the south city. During the trip, you'll get to see how some of the canal locks work.

 Scan for things to see, do and try in Dublin

WICKLOW

NATURE | GARDENS | NATIONAL PARK

Experience
Wicklow
online

Wicklow National Park

Naas

Explore the gardens and tour the distillery at **Powerscourt House & Gardens** (p85)
⏱ ½ day

Glencree

Blessington

Poulaphouca Reservoir

Admire lake views on a tour of **Russborough House & Parklands** (p86)
⏱ ½ day

Forage for fruits, nuts and mushrooms on a **guided walk** (p89)
⏱ ½ day

KILDARE

WICKLOW

Find forest glens and a waterfall in **Glenmalure Valley** (p93)
⏱ 1 day

Laragh

Drumgoff

WICKLOW
TRIP BUILDER

Catch your breath on a summit hike up **Lugnaquilla** (p93)
⏱ 8 hr

▬▬▬ Walk in a forest, stroll the gardens of a stately home or climb a mountain for rewarding views – there's plenty to keep you busy in Wicklow, known as 'the Garden of Ireland'. Immerse yourself in gorgeous landscapes or take to the coast for refreshing coastal walks and golden beaches.

Explore bookable experiences in Wicklow online

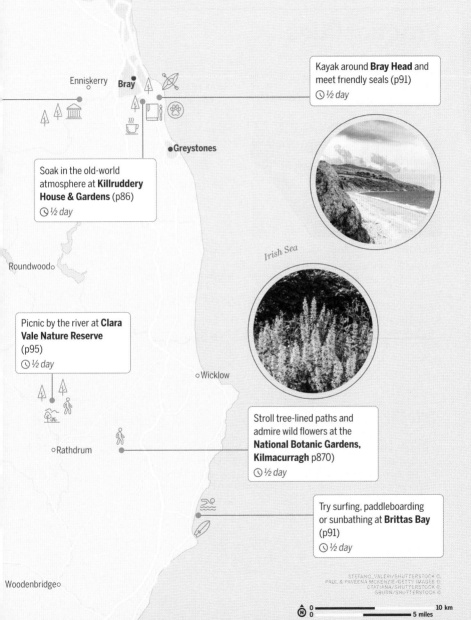

Kayak around **Bray Head** and meet friendly seals (p91)
🕐 ½ day

Enniskerry

Bray

●Greystones

Soak in the old-world atmosphere at **Killruddery House & Gardens** (p86)
🕐 ½ day

Roundwood○

Irish Sea

Picnic by the river at **Clara Vale Nature Reserve** (p95)
🕐 ½ day

○ Wicklow

○Rathdrum

Stroll tree-lined paths and admire wild flowers at the **National Botanic Gardens, Kilmacurragh** p870)
🕐 ½ day

Try surfing, paddleboarding or sunbathing at **Brittas Bay** (p91)
🕐 ½ day

Woodenbridge○

🧭 N   0 _____ 10 km
        0 _____ 5 miles

Practicalities

ARRIVING

By train The DART runs from Dublin to Bray and Greystones and there are Irish Rail trains to Wicklow, Rathdrum and Arklow. From here, connect to local buses or taxi.

By car The M11 motorway runs south through County Wicklow. If driving directly to Glendalough, note that car parks can fill up early on weekends and bank holidays.

WHEN TO GO

JAN - MAR

Chilly, short days but evenings brighter towards spring.

APR - JUN

Warmer, drier days and bursts of colour in gardens. Be prepared for showers.

JUL - SEP

Warmest and driest in July and August.

OCT - DEC

Much cooler, but beautiful autumn colours in the forests.

HOW MUCH FOR A

Surf lesson
€45

Whiskey tasting
€25

Gardens entry
€8.50

GETTING AROUND

Train Services run mostly along the coast.

Bus Services exist between the main towns, but it is not easy to get between the attractions using public transport.

Car The best way to get around; popular spots get busy with day-trippers from Dublin at weekends and holidays.

EATING & DRINKING

Organic This is the garden of Ireland – go organic at the Strawberry Tree (P97) or try foraging for wild food with Wicklow Wild Foods (P89).

Cookery schools Learn to cook seasonal local dishes at Ballyknocken (P97) or cook on an open fire with Tipi Adventures (p89).

Best whiskey tasting
Powerscourt Distillery (p89)

Must-try berry wine
Wicklow Way Wines (p89)

CONNECT & FIND YOUR WAY

Wi-fi Available free of charge in most cafes, restaurants and accommodations. 4G mobile coverage is generally good but may be patchy in the mountains.

Navigation Plan your driving routes in advance as many of the roads are small. There are companies providing baggage shuttles if you're walking the Wicklow Way.

WHERE TO STAY

Place	Pro/Con
Glendalough	Peaceful village setting; direct access to scenic Glendalough Valley.
Ashford	Sleeping options like Tinakilly Country House, with gardens and sea views, Hunter's Hotel or Ballyknocken House.
Enniskerry	Gorgeous village, adjacent to the Powerscourt Estate and waterfall.
Dunlavin	This is where you'll find Rathsallagh House, set on 500 acres with thousands of trees.
Macreddin Village	Check into BrookLodge for organic food, golf and pub in a quiet, countryside setting.

WICKLOW PASSPORT

Keep track of the places you visit with a Wicklow Passport (€2), which can be stamped in towns and villages across the county (visitwicklow.ie/passport).

MONEY

Credit and debit cards are widely accepted. Bring any cash you need in advance as you may not find ATMs easily.

07

Gardens &
HOMES

GARDENS | NATURE | DAY TRIPS

County Wicklow is a nature lover's delight and a stroll around some of its stately homes and gardens is a lovely, calming experience. Feel the weight of history in grand formal gardens, wander among ancient oaks and admire swaying wild-flower meadows.

 How to

Getting around
Powerscourt (Enniskerry village) and Killruddery (around 2.5km from Bray) are served by buses. Russborough House (Blessington) has limited bus access and you'll need a car to get to Kilmacurragh.

When to go Spring for rhododendrons, summer for wildflowers, autumn for colour. In good weather, the gardens get packed with Dubliners on day trips.

Time for tea All of the gardens have cafes for post-stroll refreshments.

Aristocratic grandeur One of the county's grandest mansions and gardens is **Powerscourt House & Gardens** (powerscourt.com), set on a magnificent estate overlooking the Wicklow countryside and the Sugarloaf Mountain. The house and gardens date back to 1730 and the 47 acres includes formal walks, walled gardens and a Japanese garden, as well as a terrace cafe and distillery.

'Powerscourt is the aristocratic garden. You've got huge urns, enormous fountains, Victorian wrought-iron railings and ornate gates,' says Seamus O'Brien, head gardener at the National Botanic Gardens in Kilmacurragh. 'Powerscourt is remarkable for its trees – the towering giant redwoods and beech trees. There's a beech avenue that sweeps up from the incredibly ornate gateway. In autumn, those beech trees turn russet and it's just beautiful.'

Best of the Rest

Other great Wicklow houses, parks and gardens include **Avondale House & Forest Park** for woodland walks or historic house tours; **Glendalough** in the Wicklow Mountains National Park for lakes, walks and a 6th-century monastic village; and **Mount Usher Gardens** in Ashford for riverside walks and carpets of spring blooms.

Left Glendalough
Above left Powerscourt House & Gardens
Above right Russborough House

Old-world ambience Set on an 800-acre estate and dating to the 1640s, **Killruddery House & Gardens** (killruddery.com) has one of the oldest and last-remaining Dutch-style gardens in Ireland and Britain. The estate is home to the Earl and Countess of Meath and has been in the Brabazon family since 1618. You can take a tour of the house, and there's a working farm with a farm shop, a cafe, a tea room, and an excellent year-round Saturday farmers market.

'If you walk the canals, you can look out over the ha-ha, a sunken ditch. It meant you didn't need a fence so the landscape was uninterrupted,' says Seamus. 'You have this lovely Elizabethan revival house with a much earlier garden surrounding it, and then this grand perspective leading away from it.'

Views Another grand Wicklow stately home is **Russborough House & Parklands** (russborough.ie), where you can tour the 1740s Palladian mansion and admire its art

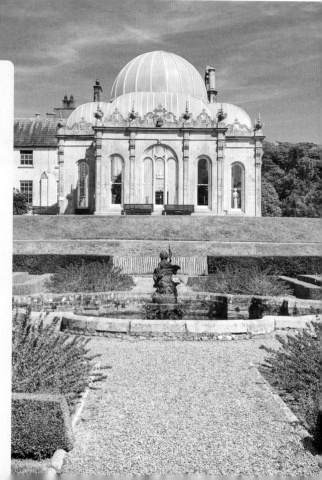

🌿 A Garden Lover's Tips

If you love giant trees, head to **Powerscourt**, which includes the tallest tree in Ireland (a 61.5m Douglas fir) and miles of stately beech trees.

Killruddery has miles of tree-lined walks and a conservatory filled with marble statues gathered from a former Earl of Meath's Grand Tour. The beech and hornbeam hedges turn russet colour in autumn and are magical.

Mount Usher is lovely in spring for naturalised bulbs. Alpine squills, a spring bulb, turn the lawns blue in places.

Recommended by Seamus O'Brien, head gardener, National Botanic Gardens, Kilmacurragh

Kilbride ○
Enniskerry
● Bray
Powerscourt House
& Gardens
Killruddery House
& Gardens
Russborough House
& Parklands
Powerscourt
Distillery
● Greystones
Blessington Lake
Poulaphouca
Reservoir
W I C K L O W
○ Roundwood
Wicklow
Mountains
Ashford ○
Mount Usher
Sugarloaf
Mountain
○ Wicklow
Glenealy ○
National Botanic
Gardens
(Kilmacurragh)
Rathdrum ○
0   10 km
0   5 miles

Left Killruddery House & Gardens
Below Mount Usher gardens

collection, or explore the grounds and walking trails, enjoying views over the lakes of Blessington and the Wicklow Mountains.

'What's lovely about Russborough is the historic landscape the house sits so comfortably in – the huge beech trees, the views of the Blessington Lake and the classical facade of the magnificent manor house,' says Seamus. 'It is wonderful in spring for bulbs and the secret Spring Garden is full of wonderful rhododendrons.'

Wild flowers The original house and early gardens at the **National Botanic Gardens, Kilmacurragh** (botanicgardens.ie) date from 1697 and the comparatively modern, wild garden was created in the 1850s. The house is yet to be restored, but you can walk among 150-year-old oriental spruces or Japanese red cedars, or an ancient avenue of yew trees.

There are free garden tours and as well as carpets of pink petals in spring from the Himalayan rhododendrons, you can see Chilean myrtles with rust-coloured barks, King Billy pines from Tasmania and 30ft fuchsias from New Zealand. 'I really like the wildness of the garden,' says Seamus. 'We don't have closely cropped lawns, we have wild-flower meadows with thousands of wild orchids in summertime. It's a wild, romantic garden.'

08
The Garden of
IRELAND

FOOD | DRINK | NATURE

▬▬▬ Wicklow's enchanting scenery has earned it a nickname as 'the Garden of Ireland', but its lush green landscape is more than just a pretty picture: some of Ireland's finest food is harvested from the county's fertile hills and meadows, and is lovingly crafted by local producers. You can sample wild berry wines, take a distillery tour or taste wild food on a foraging walk.

FOTOGRAFIE.SCHMIDT/SHUTTERSTOCK ©

🗺 **How to**

Getting here Hiring a car is best as public transport is limited, usually requiring multiple bus journeys.

When to go Spring is the best time to see Wicklow's bright yellow gorse and abundance of wild flowers. Autumn is best for foraging wild mushrooms.

Scenic train ride If you've lots of spare time take the DART from Dublin along the coast to the pretty seaside town of Greystones, then local buses or taxis from there.

ROMAN OVERKO/SHUTTERSTOCK ©

DIRK HUDSON/SHUTTERSTOCK ©

Nature's pantry Take a foraging walk along quiet country lanes with local expert Geraldine Kavanagh from **Wicklow Wild Foods** (wicklowwildfoods.com) who honed her skills in the hills surrounding her Wicklow home. Learn how to identify and cook with truly organic, wild seasonal feasts of local fruits, flowers, nuts and an array of mushrooms and tender leaves. Visit in spring and Geraldine will share her recipes for gorse-flower ice cream and wild garlic pesto.

Wild wines Irish berries are the superstars at **Wicklow Way Wines** (wicklowwaywines.ie). Pamela and Brett have brought their passion for Irish food and nature into handcrafting award-winning wines, using the finest locally grown fruits. Brett will guide you through the winery from pressing fruit to processing in their production room. Afterwards, sample strawberry, blackberry and raspberry wines with perfectly paired Irish cheeses and chocolates.

Whiskey and history The whiskey tasting at **Powerscourt Distillery** (powerscourtdistillery.com) is far from typical. Santina Kennedy has brought her expertise and passion for the history of Irish food to the Fercullen, Food and Folklore tour, where Fercullen Whiskey is paired with local wild and artisan foods (ask Santina for her wild berry cocktail recipes). Fercullen was the ancient Gaelic name given to these lands where the whiskey's barley is now sowed. The Old Mill House, the estate's historic hub of farming, houses part of the distillery.

Left Powerscourt Distillery **Far left top** Wild cooking demonstration **Far left bottom** Seasonal berries

Best Food Experiences

Wild cooking Go wild camping in the woods with Tipi Adventures (tipiadventures.ie), where you'll feast on wild and local food, such as traditional, grass-fed Wicklow lamb, cooked on an open fire. Learning the art of wild cooking is part of Tipi's bush craft courses, hosted in a tranquil forest by the River Avonmore.

Food festivals At the end of June or beginning of July, there's Taste of Wicklow (tasteofwicklow.ie), the biggest foodie event of the year. During the October bank holiday weekend there's October Feast (wicklownaturally.ie/events). In winter, tuck into artisan food and craft beers at the Christmas Market (wicklowchristmasmarket.com).

09 Seaside **VENTURES**

ADVENTURE | OUTDOORS | BEACH

Wicklow may be known for its mountains and fertile fields, but it's also blessed with a beautiful coastline of long sandy beaches, hidden coves and sheltered harbours. Calm waters create the perfect environment for fun-filled adventures such as diving off rocks, exploring caves by kayak or surfing and balancing on an SUP like a pro. Seals and dolphins regularly pop up to visit.

🗺 **How to**

Getting here/around Bray and Wicklow are easily accessed by public transport from Dublin but you need to drive to Brittas Bay.

When to go Summertime means warmer weather but also school holidays, so it gets very busy on the coast. If you're not used to swimming in cold water, July and August are best.

Thar she blows Peak season for wildlife is June to September, with sightings of dolphins and minke whales.

Left Sea kayaking, Bray **Far left top** Brittas Bay **Far left bottom** Grey seal

Sea kayaking Suitable for everyone from beginners to seasoned paddlers, sea kayaking with **Bray Adventures** (brayadventures.ie) is a great way to experience Wicklow's secret coves. Try a taster session in the safety of Bray Harbour to learn the basics. If the sea is rough, classes are held in the tranquil Dargle River by the harbour. Their expert guides can take you on a wild coastal kayak tour beneath **Bray Head**, where you'll meet curious seals and learn about migrating species at the nearby protected bird sanctuary.

Coasteering Cliff jumping, caving and sea swimming your way around some of Wicklow's coastal hidden gems is a guaranteed adrenaline rush. **Bray Adventures** are the only coasteering operators in Dublin and Wicklow – they know the best spots.

Surf's up One of the finest Blue Flag beaches in the country is **Brittas Bay**, a 5km golden stretch suitable for both swimmers and surfers. Beginners can learn with **Brittas Bay Surf School** (brittasbaysurfschool.com) and more experienced surfers take on the offshore waves solo with two-hour surf rentals. The school's kids camps are great fun, with beach games and gentle waves to learn on.

Boat trips Head out to sea on an angling adventure with **Wicklow Boat Charters** (wicklowboatcharters.ie). Common catches include smooth hound, pollock, dog fish and mackerel. Or just chill out on a scenic boat trip to take in historic sights and marine life.

Surfing & SUP: Local Tips

Manager at Brittas Bay Surf School, Hugh Arthur (@hugharthur) has been surfing for 30 years. One of his favourite spots to surf is **Magheramore Beach** – a much smaller, less well known beach than Brittas Bay. Here, the tides and weather can create the perfect combination for swells suitable for intermediate surfers.

Hugh recommends the trip from **Wicklow Harbour** to **Wicklow Lighthouse** as one of the county's finest SUP experiences. There's strong tidal currents so you need to be experienced to do it alone. Alternatively, Hugh leads tours along this gorgeous stretch of coast.

10

Wandering
WICKLOW

OUTDOORS | HIKING | NATURE

From climbing the highest peak in the region, to scenic hikes above ancient glacial valleys, secluded woodland strolls or coastal trails, Wicklow is a walker's paradise. Its close proximity to Dublin makes it easily accessible even on a day trip.

🗺 How to

Getting here Hiring a car is the best option. Most trailheads are not serviced by public transport, but there is a service to Glendalough Valley (glendalough bus.com).

When to go Summer days are ideal, but be prepared for busy trails. Spring and autumn are quieter and bring bursts of colour.

What to pack Sometimes it's four seasons in one day – pack layers, rain gear and sturdy walking boots.

Wilderness & Waterfalls

The 20km-long **Glenmalure Valley** is wonderfully wild and remote, and it's easy to see how Irish rebels used the rugged terrain to hold off English troops for centuries. A rebel memorial and the remains of historic lead mines are within walking distance of Baravore Carpark. From here, there's a short (3km) but steep trail through **Baravore Forest** to **Fraughan Rock Glen** and waterfall, an enchanting place with a fairy-tale setting and incredible shades of green. Keep an eye out for feral goats, descendants of the lead mines' herd.

Take the short Miner's Path from **Ballinafunshogue Waterfall** for sweeping views across the valley and cascading **Carrowaystick Waterfall** (spot the whitewashed stone cottage at its base, once a rebel safe house). This steep trail joins the **Wicklow Way**, one of

⛰ Lofty Peak

Leinster's highest mountain, **Lugnaquilla** (925m), is a strenuous but rewarding climb (five to eight hours). The weather is changeable, so only experienced hikers should attempt it solo. If hiring a local guide, make sure they have the accredited Mountain Leader Qualification.

Recommended by Russell Mills, guide at Mountaintrails @mnttrailsie

Left Lugnaquilla **Above left** Glendalough Valley (p94) **Above right** Lough Tay (p94)

Europe's best multiday hikes. From here it's 14km to Glendalough, one of the easier (and most scenic) sections of the Wicklow Way. Hiking gear essential.

Bird's-Eye Views

The colour-coded routes in **Glendalough Valley** are easy to follow. **The Spinc** ridge, a 3½-hour strenuous, uphill hike, is busy but worth it for its dramatic viewing point 500m above the lakes. Keep an eye out for herds of sika deer.

One of the most accessible summits is **Djouce Mountain** (725m). Park at JB Malone Memorial car park. After a short (300m) steep climb to the memorial for views of **Lough Tay**, the summit is 8km further, mostly along a boardwalk. The panorama spans 360 degrees. Boots and warm layers are essential.

Secret Valleys

Some lesser known but no less beautiful trails are to be found in Wicklow's secluded valleys

♨ Post-Hike Therapy

From September to April, in a meadow opposite **Glenmalure Lodge** (good for fireside pints and delicious food), there's an outdoor wood-fired sauna on the banks of the River Avonbeg for walkers to soothe their tired bodies after a long day's hike. After sweating in the **Bosca Beatha** (boscabeatha.ie), experience total connection with nature by dipping into the cool, clear plunge pool that's fed by the river. For an extra stretch of those muscles, take a yoga class inside Bosca Beatha's Yurt Space with energy practitioner Shirley Fitzpatrick. It's advisable to book both online in advance.

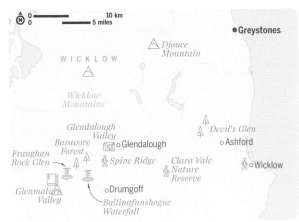

WICKLOW EXPERIENCES

Left Clara Vale Nature Reserve **Below** Wicklow Head Lighthouse

filled with ancient woodland and host to an abundance of wildlife. **Devil's Glen** has an enchanting woodland trail (4km) that follows the words of the poet Seamus Heaney and has sculptures by world-renowned artists. Follow the **Waterfall Walk** (5km) to the powerful Devil's Glen Waterfall.

Riverside hikes The Avonmore Way (An Abhainn Mhór is Irish for 'big river') is a 12km hike that traverses **Clara Vale Nature Reserve**. At the reserve entrance, around 200m north of the stone-arched Clara Vale Bridge, there's also a couple of easy looped walks ranging from 2km to 9.5km, colour-coded for easy navigation. The reserve includes some of Ireland's few remaining oak stands. Pack a picnic for a tranquil rest beside the slow-moving Avonmore, where hot tired feet can be dipped into the cool clear waters.

Coastal trails A short train ride from Dublin, the 7km **Bray to Greystones Cliff Walk** is perfect for a sunny day trip with sea views and delicious food – try the Happy Pear (p96) in Greystones. Sections of the walk may close occasionally due to coastal erosion, so be sure to follow detour signposts. The more rugged **Glen Beach Cliff Walk** (4km) from south of Wicklow Town to historic Wicklow Head Lighthouse, takes in secret coves and a seal colony. Sometimes it's also possible to spot dolphins. Proper footwear is essential as the trail can get mucky.

Listings

BEST OF THE REST

Fresh-Air Attractions

Wicklow Mountains National Park

Explore a walking trail, climb a mountain, see wildlife, stroll around a lake or take a scenic drive in this beautiful national park.

Glendalough Monastic Settlement

This peaceful settlement at Glendalough dates back to the 6th century and includes a round tower and the ruins of a cathedral and stone churches, plus old gravestones.

Sally Gap

Drive the R115, known as the Old Military Rd, to pass Sally Gap. You'll traverse some of the wildest, most scenic landscape in the county.

Greenan Maze

Get lost in a 7ft-high maze covering half an acre, or try the solstice maze for a more meditative experience. There's also a farm, farm museum and fairy-tree walk.

Active Adventures

Wicklow Way

Take six or seven days to walk this 129km route from Marlay Park in South County Dublin to Clonegal in County Carlow, passing through some of Wicklow's most spectacular scenery.

Ballinastoe Mountain Bike Trail

The forest here, just north of Roundwood, has 14km of demanding MTB trails, some which come out at spectacular views over Lough Tay.

Brennanstown Riding School

Take a horse-riding lesson, or try a scenic cross-country trek from Brennanstown through some of the County Wicklow countryside on a half- or full-day excursion.

Tour Around

Day Trips

There are lots of tour companies that will bring you on a day trip by bus to Glendalough, Avoca village and through the Wicklow Mountains from Dublin city centre, usually leaving from Dublin city's O'Connell St.

Wicklow Gaol

You might meet some interesting characters when exploring the Gaol – take the Gates of Hell virtual reality tour or a night tour if you are brave enough.

Animal Encounters

Glenroe Farm

Have fun with rabbits and guinea pigs in the pet farm, learn about the bigger farm animals, take a nature walk or try the maze.

K2 Alpacas

Take a walk with a friendly alpaca in Newtownmountkennedy. As you learn about these curious animals, you'll hear them humming to each other.

Sealife

Get up close and personal with some friendly rays, find out how sharks start life in special pouches, gawp at clownfish and more in this great aquarium on Bray's seafront.

Tasty Treats

Happy Pear €

Get a dose of positivity at this wholefood cafe and shop in Greystones, set up by twins Dave and Steve, who are passionate about plant-based food.

Firehouse Bakery €

This artisan bakery in Delgany turns out all types of fresh bread and pastries from its wood stove every morning – try the ice cream during summer season.

Platform Pizza Bar €

Tuck into a slow-roast pulled-pork pizza or a vegan special on a spelt base, and sip a Bray Bré cocktail in this popular spot in Bray town.

Burrito Box €

Sizzling burritos, nachos and sweet potato fries are conjured up and served from this food truck at the Boatyard in Greystones.

Country Cooking

Hunter's Hotel €€€

This old-style family-run hotel in Rathnew is open for breakfast, lunch, dinner and after-noon tea – enjoy a stroll in the gardens.

Strawberry Tree €€€

Have a fully organic meal at Brooklodge hotel's restaurant in Macreddin Village, with lots sourced or foraged locally – peek into its pantry, which is a treasure trove of wild foods.

Ballyknocken Cookery School €€€

Learn to make your own dish in the setting of this country house, run by TV chef Catherine Fulvio, using ingredients from the garden.

Poppies €

Gorgeous home-style country cooking in Enniskerry village. Pop in for tea and cakes, a light lunch or a filling quiche or pie.

Irish Gifts & Local Treasures

Avoca

Browse for Irish gifts and homewares such as luxury throws, candles, cookbooks and crafts. The Kilmacanogue emporium also has a food market, cafe and the Fern House restaurant.

Greenan Maze

Fishers

This family-run shop in Newtownmount-kennedy is the place to stock up on country casual clothing. You will also find Irish gifts and there's also a shop selling local produce.

Tinahely Farm Shop

There's lots to do here. Have a look around the food and gift shop – there's also a restaurant, farm animals and a children's activity barn.

Boat Yard Gallery

Pick some local art and photography in this gallery, set in the small Boat Yard courtyard near Greystones Harbour.

Craft Tipples

Wicklow Wolf

Look out for IPAs and the smokey bacon-flavoured Ranchero Rauchbier from this Wicklow craft brewery, served in many of the county's pubs and off-licences.

Glendalough Distillery

Seasonal botanical gins made from wild in-gredients foraged from Wicklow's forests. This distillery also produces whiskey aged in casks made from sustainably sourced, local oak.

 Scan for things to see, do and try in Wicklow

PETER KROCKA/SHUTTERSTOCK ©

THE SOUTHEAST

BEACHES | ADVENTURE | SPORTS

Saltee Islands

THE SOUTHEAST
Trip Builder

Sandy adventures, city festivals and fun-filled family days await in the Southeast. Catch a hurling match or soak up medieval history in Kilkenny, explore Waterford's glorious Unesco geopark, then hit the beaches in Wexford.

Castlecomer ○

Catch a hurling match in **Kilkenny city**, home of the Cats (p112)
🕓 ½ day

Kilkenny ●

○ Cashel

TIPPERARY

● **Tipperary**

● **Clonmel**

Knockanaffrin ⛰

WATERFORD

Explore geographical wonders at the Unesco **Copper Coast Geopark** (p116)
🕓 1 day

See what's in bloom or rent the historic **Lismore Castle** (p120)
🕓 1-2 days

 ● Lismore

Bunmahon ○ ●

Dungarvan
○ *Dungarvan Harbour*

CORK

•Carlow

Ride the zipline and take a treetop walk at **Castlecomer Discovery Park** (p111)
🕐 1 day

Climb the cliffs then go for a swim at **Ballymoney Beach** (p105)
🕐 1 day

C A R L O W

W E X F O R D

○Courtown

Mt Leinster △

Discover why **Curracloe Beach** was so important to Steven Spielberg (p108)
🕐 ½ day

I L K E N N Y

○Blackwater

Wexford Bay

Curracloe ○

•New Ross

Hike over golden sand dunes on the **Furlongs Road Loop** (p106)
🕐 ½ day

Wexford *Wexford Harbour*

Experience the southern sunset by kayak around **Hook Head** (p107)
🕐 ½ day

Duncormick ○

○Rosslare Harbour

Waterford

St George's Channel

Ballyteige Bay

○Kilmore Quay

Sail to the rugged **Saltee Islands** (p107)
🕐 1 day

Waterford Harbour

Churchtown ○

Celtic Sea

N 0   20 km
   0   10 miles

Practicalities

ARRIVING

Kilkenny MacDonagh Train Station Direct connections to Waterford; buses park outside.

Wexford O'Hanrahan Railway Station Direct routes from Dublin, with a stop for Rosslare Strand beach.

Waterford Plunkett Train Station Five-minute walk to city centre.

HOW MUCH FOR A

99 ice cream
€2

Hurling match ticket €35

Pint of Smith-wicks €4.50

GETTING AROUND

Car The most convenient way to get around, and a popular way to explore the Southeast coast while beach-hopping.

Train Connections from Dublin to Kilkenny city, Waterford city and Wexford towns. Bear in mind that there's only one Waterford stop, so you may need to get a bus or a taxi to more remote areas.

WHEN TO GO

JAN - MAR
Cool, fresh weather. Ideal for city breaks and inland exploring.

APR - JUN
Warmer days. Beach and tourist season building up.

JUL - SEP
Mostly warm weather. Busy coast in July.

OCT - DEC
Expect colder, wetter days. Snuggle up by the fire.

THE SOUTHEAST FIND YOUR FEET

EATING & DRINKING

Jackford Potato Gin Delightful, earthy potato-based spirit from Enniscorthy.

Blaa Special, doughy, white Waterford bread. Protected Geographical Indication status by the European Commission. Try in Barron's Bakery, Cappoquin.

Must-try black pudding Anocht (p121) in Kilkenny specialises in modern Irish cuisine and serves an excellent black pudding terrine.

Best ice cream 99s and whipped sundaes at Henry's in Campile (p105).

CONNECT & FIND YOUR WAY

Wi-fi Wi-fi and 4G phone coverage is generally good across Kilkenny, Wexford and Waterford. Connectivity is set to further improve when a new high-speed fibre broadband network is rolled out to rural locations.

Navigation Maps, guides and traveller information are available in tourism offices in Kilkenny, Waterford and Wexford towns.

WHERE TO STAY

Place	Pro/Con
Waterford City	Hotels and guesthouses on the river. Tourist hotspot, book early.
Kilkenny City	Hostels to luxury hotels. Hen party capital of Ireland; noisy.
Rosslare	Beachside, best for families & walkers. Popular, but limited accommodation.
Nire Valley	Eco-camping and glamping. Public transport limited.

MONEY

Cash and cards are both widely accepted in towns and cities. Bring cash for ice creams by the beach.

FOOD THE WATERFORD WAY

Find the location of local food producers, restaurants, food stores and farmers markets on the Food the Waterford Way map (foodthewaterfordway.com).

11

Wexford Beach
LIFE

FAMILY | ADVENTURE | COAST

Famous for its superb beaches, Wexford is worthy of time spent acquainting yourself with its coastline. The area has some of the cleanest strands in all of Ireland – perfect for family days out and some R&R.

🗺 How to

Getting here Travel to Wexford from Dublin by car (less than two hours) for easy beach access, or take the train direct to Rosslare Strand.

When to go Wexford is called the 'Sunny Southeast' for a reason: it has many sunshine hours throughout the year. May/June is ideal for sunbathing on the beaches.

Best dunes Visit Ballyteige Burrow to see one of the best sand dune systems in Ireland.

Sandy days out Visit **Kilgorman Strand** and soak in the 2.5km full length of the beach, which includes the soft sands of **Clone Strand**. There is no carpark here, so locals tend to park along the road to access it. The beach is wide with plenty of space for families to lounge and swim in the ocean.

Go swimming at **Ballymoney Beach**. This popular, safe, bathing spot has lifeguards during peak season (July to August) as well as access to public toilets. If visiting in summer, head down early to nab a parking spot.

Further south, the unspoilt **Duncannon Beach** (just outside the village) is a joy on a warm day. There's parking at the water's edge or you can drive onto the golden sand. The beach has great views of Hook Head and hosts an annual Sand Sculpting Festival (early August).

🍨 Cool as Ice

Wexford's coastal vibes go hand in hand with ice-cream blowouts. Locals love the 99s and whipped sundaes from Henry's in Campile, or try locally made Scúp gelato from Bella Napoli in Kilmuckridge. If you're taking a stroll on Rosslare Strand, nab a delicious tub or cone at Izmoo Gelato.

Left Ballymoney Beach **Above left** Morriscastle Beach (p106) **Above right** Hook Lighthouse

Known as the 'Golden Mile', the glorious **Morriscastle Beach** in Kilmuckridge is also lifeguarded during peak season. Morriscastle is a clean, family-friendly beach bordered by dunes that provide welcome shelter from the breeze.

Active adventures Pull on a wetsuit and take to the water on a stand-up paddleboard (SUP) or try a kitesurfing lesson with Hooked Kite Surfing (hookedkitesurfing.ie). The company's base, Duncannon Beach, hosts

Wexford's annual Hooked Kitefest each August.

Take a hike Wexford's great walks include the 4.5km **Furlongs Road Loop**, where you can take pathways along the beach or through the dunes. The higher dunes have incredible views of the entire area, including **Ballyteige Castle** and **Forth Mountain**.

Wexford from the Water

For one of the best coastal experiences

👪 Best Family Experiences

Curracloe Strand Take surf lessons at Surf Shack or hike and bike the walking trail at Ravenwood through the forest to the beach.

Duncannon Beach Shallow water and lifeguards mean a safe swim. For younger children there's a great playground just off the beach in the dunes.

Ballymoney Beach Explore the rockpools between the two beaches and climb the cliffs for amazing views – you can see all the way to Wales on a clear day.

Carne Beach Go horse riding on the beach with Hazelwood Stables.

Recommended by Sinéad Fox, mum and blogger at BumblesofRice.com @bumblesofrice

Wexford has to offer, head to Fethard-on-Sea village and join a **sunset kayaking tour** with The Irish Experience (theirishexperience.com). You'll be accompanied by a local guide, who will lead a paddle around the Hook Head coastline to explore sea caves, arches and glorious sea cliffs. Curious seals may join in the fun, and if you're really lucky you might even spot dolphins and basking sharks while pottering about this impressive habitat. Afterwards, you'll be plied with hot chocolate while bobbing on the water, with a front-row seat to see the sun sink beneath the horizon. You'll need at least three hours for the evening out.

Sailing Great Saltee Take a **family sailing trip** with Saltee Ferry (salteeferry.com). Just 5km from Kilmore Quay, the islands are home to an array of birds such as guillemots and razorbills. Colourful **puffins** arrive in April and stay until mid-August. Plan a trip in early summer to enjoy a sea of bluebells.

If you prefer to keep your feet on terra firma, The Irish Experience also runs self-guided cycle tours and hiking experiences around Wexford. For something more adventurous, there's also coastal canyoneering.

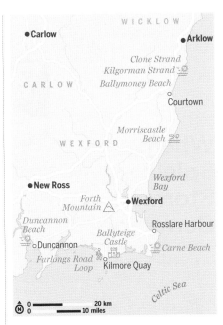

THE SOUTHEAST EXPERIENCES

Left Carne Beach **Right** Puffin, Saltee Islands

When Spielberg Stormed Curracloe

AN EXTRA'S INSIGHT TO THE HOLLYWOOD BLOCKBUSTER

In the summer of 1997, a sandy strand in County Wexford was transformed into Normandy's Omaha Beach and featured in what is perhaps one of the greatest opening scenes of any WWII movie. A massive success, *Saving Private Ryan* brought in £4 million to the Wexford economy and left a lasting legacy.

Left and right Scenes from the 1998 film *Saving Private Ryan* **Middle** Curracloe Beach

When Steven Spielberg chose Curracloe Strand for the D-Day scenes in his wartime epic *Saving Private Ryan*, it may have been a surprising choice to many, but locals knew the value of this stretch of sand. Running for 11km, the beach is popular with locals for bracing walks, but for Spielberg its size meant ample room to play out the large-scale, tense D-Day landings of 1944. The scenes shot on Curracloe Strand replay the fateful attack by US infantry, who landed at Normandy's Omaha Beach in their thousands in an effort to quash German artillery on the beach heights, creating a giant killing zone.

More than 1000 extras were used on Curracloe. Tipperary-man Mick Delahunty, a former member of the FCA (An Fórsa Cosanta Áitiúil; now the Reserve Defence Forces), was one of them, and remembers it well. He spent 4½ weeks on set in one of the core army groups, working closest with the main cast. Spielberg's team approached the Irish army to recruit extras because of their experience of conflict and their discipline, according to Mick. 'They wanted people who knew what to do,' he says – capturing the tension and bleakness of WWII was no easy feat.

For Mick's audition, he had to swim lengths of a pool wearing a tracksuit to see how he would cope with potential conditions. Extras were bused down to the beach each day and they also had a historian on set who told them exactly what they were doing to simulate the D-Day landings. Although Irish summers typically have their fair share of cloudy days, to Spielberg's dismay 1997 was a sunny year. To emulate the grim reality of those war days

in Normandy, the director was forced to resort to lighting fires to add murkiness to the filming.

Like any Hollywood set, there was an emphasis on secrecy and some of the extras were sent home after getting caught with cameras. It was only on the last day of shooting that Mick says extras were told, 'Look, guys, we know you don't have cameras, but if you just happen to have one by accident...' He adds: 'You'd want to see the amount of cameras that came out of people's pockets!' Photographs that Mick took that day, including one of him with Tom Hanks, are now proudly on display in the Templemore Arms Hotel in County Tipperary.

> Spielberg's team approached the Irish army to recruit extras because of their experience of conflict and their discipline

When *Saving Private Ryan* hit cinemas the following year, it grossed more than US$481 million at the box office. It was nominated for 11 Academy Awards and won five, including one for Spielberg for Best Director. The film's harrowing Omaha Beach scenes are considered one of the closest film adaptations of the real-life experiences of the Normandy landings, and remain highly influential.

As well as *Saving Private Ryan*, Mick has been an extra on *Braveheart* and *The Last Duel*, and can now say that he's worked with Spielberg, Mel Gibson and Ridley Scott. 'Not bad for a lad that's only an extra!' he jokes.

Real-Life Curracloe

This wonderful sandy beach was chosen for its geographical similarity to Omaha Beach. These days, it's still a local favourite with soft, fine white sand that's ideal underfoot. A blanket of green marram grass covers the surrounding sand dunes and adds to the serene atmosphere.

Curracloe Beach is well known for being particularly safe for bathers and has an International Blue Flag – awarded due to its cleanliness. Lifeguards look after swimmers during bathing season (July to August).

Parking is plentiful, with three sites to aim for: White Gap, Ballinesker and Culleton's Gap.

12

Family Thrills in
KILKENNY

NATURE | ACTIVITIES | ANIMALS

Although well known for its medieval history, Kilkenny is also a county with bountiful opportunities to be outdoors in nature. Families will love it here, where small kids can get up close and personal with farm animals or experience woodland romps, and kids big and small can run riot with ziplines, mountain biking and kayaking.

MARIUS ROMAN/GETTY IMAGES ©

🗺 How to

Getting around Having your own transport is advised, to ensure you can visit the attractions outside the city and stop for walks, picnics and photos.

When to go Many outdoor activities run year-round, but you'll get the best out of them from March to September.

Top tip If your kids like sports, they might be fascinated by the local obsession: hurling. Ask about the best upcoming matches.

BOULENGER XAVIER/SHUTTERSTOCK©

CASTLECOMER DISCOVERY PARK ©

Left Castlecomer Discovery Park
Far left top Kilkenny Castle **Far left bottom** Art installation, Kilkenny Castle

Castlecomer Discovery Park

Active families will be thrilled with the adventures on offer at Castlecomer Discovery Park (discoverypark.ie). Housed in the former grounds of the Wandesforde Estate, the park is spread over 80 acres of woodlands and lakes. Activities range from Ireland's longest zipline and treetop walks to archery, kayaking, orienteering and mountain biking.

'Seeing families connect with nature, while doing physical activity brings a smile to my face,' explains Kathy Purcell, general manager of the Discovery Park. 'This is a keystone of our philosophy.'

For the under-sevens, there is a magical elf and fairy village, bouncing net and a woodland adventure playground housed in the trees. Suitable for over-sevens, the treetop walk is a 140m-long walk in the trees, suspended 10m above the forest floor. For over-12s, the zipline is more than 300m long and crosses two lakes and a bridge. It can be booked in conjunction with the Octagon high-ropes course, which is a more challenging version of the treetop walk. All are designed to test your agility and give tremendous views over the woodland.

There is also the Castlecomer Craft Yard featuring artists, ceramicists, potters and jewellers, the Coal Mining Museum and the gastro-style family Jarrow Restaurant. Opened as a community project in 2007, Castlecomer Discovery Park attracts over 100,000 visitors each year and has won awards for Community Forestry and Social Enterprises.

The park is a 20-minute drive north of Kilkenny city.

✿ For Young Explorers

National Reptile Zoo
Learn about ecosystems and conservation in this fun, educational city setting with turtles, tarantulas, snakes and lizards.

Shenanigans Tour of Kilkenny This entertaining city walking tour along Ireland's Medieval Mile blends history with magic, featuring witches and knights.

Nore Valley Park In a peaceful valley a 15-minute drive from Kilkenny City, this pet farm offers kids the opportunity to bottle-feed baby lambs, hold piglets and interact with ostriches. Camping and glamping are also on-site.

Woodstock Gardens
Overlooking the River Nore and the beautiful village of Inistioge, a 30-minute drive southeast of Kilkenny City, these gardens make for a tranquil day out amid walled gardens, an arboretum and tree-lined avenues.

13

The Game of
HURLING

CULTURE | SPORT | ACTIVITIES

An ancient Irish sport, hurling is part of the fabric of Irish society and in Kilkenny it's a religion. The local team are known as the Cats and there's nowhere better in Ireland to catch a match or learn about hurling traditions.

RAY MCMANUS/SPORTSFILE VIA GETTY IMAGES ©

🎞 How to

Getting there Hurling pitches are dotted around the county of Kilkenny, so often a car (or bike) is required to catch matches.

When to go Local club games take place from February to November and happen in the evening midweek or at the weekend.

Catch a match There are 41 clubs and fixtures can be found at kilkennygaa.ie/fixtures-results.

RAY MCMANUS/SPORTSFILE VIA GETTY IMAGES ©

History of Hurling

Best described as a mixture of baseball and lacrosse, played with the intensity of ice hockey but on a grass pitch, hurling is likely part of the evolution of all of those sports.

The origin of hurling is steeped in Irish legend. Folklore tells that when a teenage boy called Setanta arrived late for a feast at Chulainn's castle, he found the gates already closed and the feast in full flow. To keep himself occupied on the long hike to the castle, he had been hitting a ball with a stick and then chasing after it. When Setanta arrived at the castle, Chulainn's guard dog (or the Cú in Irish) was already out patrolling the castle's perimeter and Setanta, to preserve his own life, used his stick to shoot the guard dog with his ball, killing the unfortunate hound.

MARK GUSEV/SHUTTERSTOCK ©

🐾 Catching a Live 'Clash of the Ash'

The success of hurling in Kilkenny has been founded upon club games that run throughout the spring, summer and autumn, culminating in local championship finals. All the players are amateur, despite the elevated skill levels, so the games happen outside of normal working hours.

Left Hurling goal posts **Above left and above right** Hurling matches

As punishment, Chulainn made Setanta his new guard dog, and henceforth the boy became known as Cú Chulainn. Through his act of self-defence, Setanta invented hurling. Historians argue that this legend is based on fact and occurred in the 12th century.

In rural Ireland, there is no greater honour than playing for your county or indeed winning an All-Ireland final. While hurling is played by men, the women's game, called camogie, is equally as popular and skilful. The All-Ireland finals in hurling draw the biggest crowd of any sporting event in Ireland, topping 82,000 spectators.

Experience Hurling

Kilkenny Way Specially designed for international visitors who are not familiar with Ireland's national game, the Kilkenny Way (thekilkennyway.com) is a guided two-hour tour that demonstrates hurling to novices like nothing else. You'll get the history of the game,

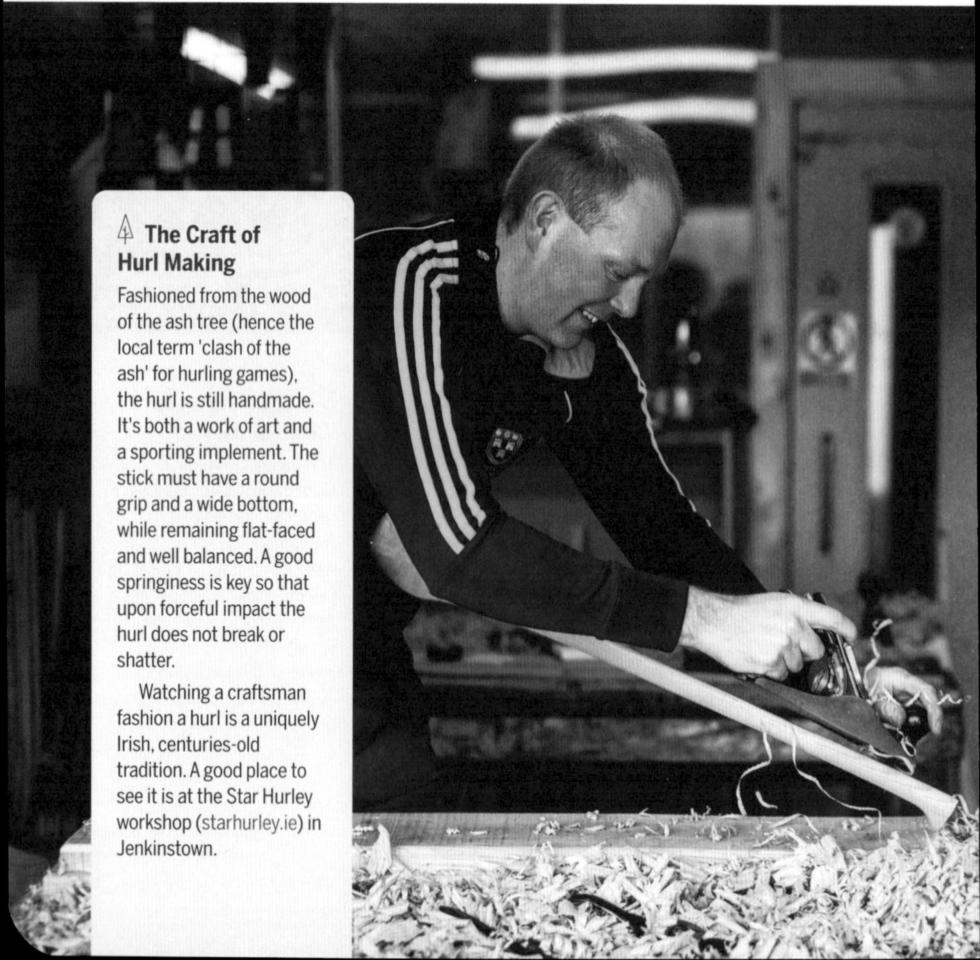

The Craft of Hurl Making

Fashioned from the wood of the ash tree (hence the local term 'clash of the ash' for hurling games), the hurl is still handmade. It's both a work of art and a sporting implement. The stick must have a round grip and a wide bottom, while remaining flat-faced and well balanced. A good springiness is key so that upon forceful impact the hurl does not break or shatter.

Watching a craftsman fashion a hurl is a uniquely Irish, centuries-old tradition. A good place to see it is at the Star Hurley workshop (starhurley.ie) in Jenkinstown.

Left Camogie match **Far left** Artisan shapes a hurl **Below** Camogie sticks

stories of local legends, and training lessons where you can learn some of the fundamental skills of hurling. You'll also get the chance to visit the home of 'the Cats' – the Kilkenny county team – at Nowlan Park stadium in Kilkenny city.

Founded on the hurling culture within Kilkenny, one of Ireland's most highly decorated counties in terms of title wins, this is an unparalleled native Kilkenny experience. The tour is run by ex-players and starts from PJ Lanigan's Bar, which also doubles as an unofficial Hurling Museum. The bar merits a visit on its own, to browse the paraphernalia and images. Excellent late-night Irish music-filled parties (nicknamed 'hoolies' by locals) abound once night falls. Book in advance.

Hands-on games For a more practical approach, book a tour through Hurling Tours Ireland (hurlingtoursireland.ie). You'll get a chance to score a point on the field of dreams after learning the history, evolution and basic skills of the world's fastest field game. A major focus is fantastic, practical and enthralling on-field lessons for all the family, provided by former club hurlers. The tour is so infectious that some international visitors have even gone home to join local Irish-run hurling clubs in their native lands after taking it. A great group activity. Book online.

Copper Coast &
MAHON FALLS

COASTAL | ACTIVE | HISTORY

▰▰▰▰ Geological formations at Waterford's Copper Coast evoke memories of the area's copper-mining heritage. Designated a Unesco Geopark, the coastline is home to a spectacular Cycling Greenway and the famed Mahon Falls are an easy and short mountain-view detour from the route. Together, they make one of the most enjoyable trips in Ireland's Southeast – whether travelling by car, on foot or by bike.

ANDREA PISTOLESI/SHUTTERSTOCK ©

🚶 Doneraile Walk

To escape the hustle and bustle of Tramore Beach on a fine day, try the Doneraile Walk. This moderate hike is generally calmer than the beach and has ample seating along the way, from where you can admire the tremendous clifftop views. It's 2km one way to Newtown Cove.

🗺 How to

Getting around The geopark can be travelled by car, by bike or on foot – or all three in parts. At O'Mahony's Pub, near Stradbally, bikes can be rented and it's a beautiful entry point to the Cycling Greenway.

When to go Warmer temperatures and drier days can be expected from April to September.

Top tip The Cycling Greenway features plenty of locations for picnics and cafe stops.

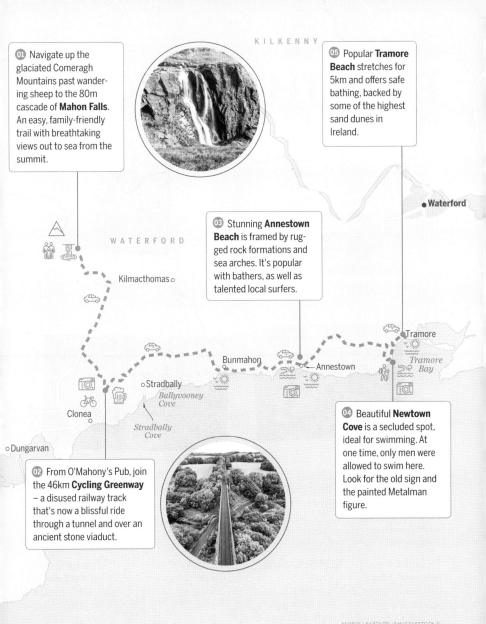

KILKENNY

01 Navigate up the glaciated Comeragh Mountains past wandering sheep to the 80m cascade of **Mahon Falls**. An easy, family-friendly trail with breathtaking views out to sea from the summit.

05 Popular **Tramore Beach** stretches for 5km and offers safe bathing, backed by some of the highest sand dunes in Ireland.

• Waterford

WATERFORD

Kilmacthomas ○

03 Stunning **Annestown Beach** is framed by rugged rock formations and sea arches. It's popular with bathers, as well as talented local surfers.

Tramore

Bunmahon

Annestown

Tramore Bay

○ Stradbally

Ballyvooney Cove

Clonea ○

Stradbally Cove

○ Dungarvan

04 Beautiful **Newtown Cove** is a secluded spot, ideal for swimming. At one time, only men were allowed to swim here. Look for the old sign and the painted Metalman figure.

02 From O'Mahony's Pub, join the 46km **Cycling Greenway** – a disused railway track that's now a blissful ride through a tunnel and over an ancient stone viaduct.

N | 0 ___ 10 km
0 ___ 5 miles

BREATHTAKING
Waterford

01 Tramore Bay
A long beach, excellent for swimming. A great viewing point is the Doneraile Walk.

02 Guillamene Swimming Cove
Safe swimming location with beautiful rocky surrounds, very popular with the locals.

03 Durrow Viaduct
Pass over this beautiful 19th-century railway viaduct as you cycle the Greenway.

04 Ballyvooney Cove
When the tide is out, look for the shipwreck on the left and explore the caves to find a secret beach.

05 Reginald's Tower
Built in the 10th century by the Vikings, this is Ireland's oldest civic building and still in continuous use.

06 Mahon Falls
The sheep here are used to such stunning vistas and the glacial-age Comeragh Mountains.

07 Newtown Cove
A special seaside picnic spot, with clifftop tables offering views across the entire Tramore Bay.

08 Crough Wood

Lovely stop-off for a
deciduous forest hill
walk in the foothills of
the Comeragh Moun-
tains, on the route to
Dungarvan.

09 Bunmahon
Ogham Stones

On display in a 'geo-
logical garden' near
Bunmahon, ancient
Ogham stones are
inscribed with primitive
writing from around the
4th century.

10 Dunmore East
Cliff Walk

Easy 2km walk offering
seascape views – you
may get lucky and see a
passing whale.

11 Greenway Tunnel

Let out a roar and hear
it echo as you cycle
through this 400m
tunnel; a highlight of the
Greenway.

Listings

BEST OF THE REST

 ### Castles, Cathedrals & Gardens

St Canice's

Built in the 13th century, this beautifully preserved cathedral in Kilkenny city features wonderful stained glass and has a round tower with fantastic views from the summit.

The Black Abbey

One of the oldest churches in Ireland, the Black Abbey has served Kilkenny city for centuries. A fantastic setting for a musical concert if your timing is right.

Kilkenny Castle

This popular attraction was built after the Norman conquest of Ireland, but then rebuilt, extended and adapted over the centuries. It's surrounded by 50 acres of park with rose gardens, woodlands and playgrounds.

Lismore Castle

A walk in the grounds of Waterford's Lismore Castle, which has two gardens dating back to the 17th century, reveals glorious plants, fragrant flowers and a working kitchen vegetable garden.

Irish National Heritage Park

This 40-acre park in Wexford features replica houses and villages of Ireland's earliest settlers.

 ### Adrenaline Rush

Axe Junkies

A fun-filled activity for adults (aged 18 and over) in Waterford city. Sling axes straight into the bullseye, in a music-filled atmosphere.

Dunmore East Adventure Centre

Located right at the water's edge where sheltered coves offer fantastic natural playgrounds, this purpose-built facility has a range of water activities as well as abseiling and archery.

Quadventure

A guaranteed day of mucky thrills and spills on four-wheels, in the foothills of Wexford's Blackstairs Mountains.

The Gap Walk

A 6km round-trip walk in the wonderful Comeragh Mountains in Waterford, through a natural pass that has been in use for centuries.

Suir Valley Railway

Take a unique and special 40-minute train trip on a narrow-gauge railway dating to 1878. It's in Waterford and the route includes fantastic river valley views.

 ### Arts & Crafts

Nicholas Mosse

Potters have worked on-site at this old stone mill, on the banks of the River Nore at Bennettsbridge, since 1840. Watch the potters work, then visit the shop and tea room.

Jerpoint Glass

In Stoneyford, visitors can watch master glassblowers magically transform molten liquid glass into intricate shapes.

Made in Kilkenny Craft Trail

Kilkenny has a long-standing reputation as a hub of creativity, which is beautifully celebrated on this craft trail featuring potters, glassblowers, metalworkers and many more besides.

The Makers House

A collection of contemporary Irish art, design and craft, all under one roof in Wexford town.

✕ Seasonal & Farm-to-Table

Everett's €€

Comfortable and unfussy, this Waterford bistro offers the best of Irish seasonal ingredients, housed in a 15th-century building.

Bodega €€

A fun, multiple award-winning dining experience in Waterford, focusing on quality local produce from the sea and the farm.

Spinnaker Bar €€

A family-friendly, nautical-themed bar and seafood restaurant in Dunmore East, with great atmosphere and service.

Anocht €€

Serving modern Irish and European cuisine, Anocht is a fine-dining experience housed in a beautiful historic room above the Kilkenny Design Centre.

Rive Gauche Kitchen & Cocktails €€

A modern take on traditional elegance, this chic and sophisticated destination in Kilkenny city centre allows the food to take centre stage.

Barrow's Keep €€€

Dedicated to local producers, this farm-to-table restaurant in Thomastown has a marvellous weekly changing menu.

Silver Fox Seafood Restaurant €€€

This Irish and seafood restaurant in Kilmore Quay, Wexford, is famous for fresh and locally caught seafood.

✕ Fine Dining

Restaurant Lady Anne €€€

An elegant and intimate Georgian dining room in the restored Creamery House at Castlecomer. Lady Anne uses local produce and offers a fantastic tasting menu.

Tannery Restaurant €€€

One of Waterford's best restaurants, in Dungarvan, with creative, delicious and attractively presented dishes.

Ristorante Rinuccini €€€

This family-owned, awarding-winning restaurant has been at the centre of Kilkenny for over 30 years, offering classic Italian fare.

Beaches Restaurant €€€

Situated in Kelly's Hotel Rosslare, this award-winning restaurant has a renowned wine list to accompany the daily changing seasonal menu.

Cheap Eats

Vee Bistro €

A relaxed and contemporary bistro in the centre of Tramore, offering Irish and European fare.

Cathedral Café €

Soups, snacks, drinks and desserts are available at this quaint cafe housed in St Mary's Cathedral, Kilkenny.

Ohana Café €

Just north of Wexford town in Fahey's Cross, this cafe features budget-friendly tasty treats. Great for lunch.

The Yard Café €

Situated in the heart of Kilkenny city, the Yard Café has access to a lot of outdoor seating and is a great spot to watch the world go by.

The Olive Café €

A great place for a traditional Irish breakfast in Waterford city.

CORK

CULTURE | HISTORY | COAST

Experience Cork online

Mizen Head

CORK
Trip Builder

Cork is the largest county in Ireland and as the locals will tell you, there's nowhere quite like it. Home to an incredible coastline, rugged natural beauty and rich, fascinating history, 'The Rebel County' has something for everyone.

KERRY

Take the cable car to **Dursey Island** and meet the resident artists (p139)
🕐 1-2 days

Make a splash with a whale-watching trip in **Baltimore** (p140)
🕐 ½ day

Glengarriff

Beara Peninsula

Allihies

Castletownbere

Bantry Bay

Bantry

Bere Island

Durrus

Kilcrohane

Drive 70km of dramatic coastline on the **Sheep's Head Peninsula** drive (p133)
🕐 1-3 days

Mizen Head Peninsula

Skibbereen

Toormore

Barleycove

Sherkin Island

Cape Clear Island

Brave the bridge-crossing at remote **Mizen Head** (p133)
🕐 ½ day

Explore bookable experiences in Cork online

N
0 —— 20 km
0 —— 10 miles

Sample local produce at **Midleton Farmers Market** (p147)
⏱ ½ day

Tour the gardens, see exotic wildlife or golf at **Fota Island** (p137)
⏱ 1 day

CORK

Kiss the stone for the 'gift of the gab' at **Blarney Castle** (p135)
⏱ ½ day

Cork

Midleton

●**Cobh**

Explore the colourful seaside town of **Kinsale**, Ireland's gourmet capital (p129)
⏱ 1 day

Kinsale

Clonakilty

Enjoy the best of **Cork city** on a self-guided walking tour (p142)
⏱ 1 day

Surf the waves or explore the dunes at **Inchydoney Beach** (p141)
⏱ ½ day

Celtic Sea

Practicalities

ARRIVING

Cork Airport 10km southwest of the city. Bus 226 connects the airport, city centre, bus and train stations hourly. Allow 20 to 35 minutes. Adult single €2.80; cash only. Taxis cost around €25. Car rental available, best booked in advance.
Kent Train Station Bus 205 connects the city centre but it's a short walk. Taxis start at €5 up to €20 for most city-centre destinations.
Cork Bus Station Located on Parnell Place in the city centre.

WHEN TO GO

JAN - MAR

Cold, dark evenings, perfect for the pub and Paddy's Day parades.

APR - JUN

Warmer weather, seasonal attractions open, Midsummer Festival.

JUL - SEP

Best weather, foodie festival Taste of West Cork.

OCT - DEC

Guinness Cork Jazz Festival and Kinsale Gourmet Festival time.

HOW MUCH FOR A

Pint of Beamish
€5

Locally roasted coffee €3.50

Potato pie
€1.80

GETTING AROUND

Bicycle Cork city is compact and very walkable, but for a change of pace there's also a bike-share system with stations at most of the city's tourist attractions. A 3-day subscription is available for €3 plus a deposit of €150. First 30 minutes free (bikeshare. ie/cork).

Bus Hop-on, hop-off bus tours of Cork city also offer day trips to Jameson Distillery, Mizen Head and the Ring of Kerry. Buses run to most major towns in Cork county. You usually have to go back to Cork city to connect.

Car The absolute best way to visit remote spots in West Cork, which can be difficult to access on public transport.

EATING & DRINKING

Breakfast Seek out Clonakilty black pudding with O'Flynn's gourmet sausages, washed down with a cup of Barry's tea.

Cheese Smoked Gubbeen, Carrigaline soft cheeses, Toonsbridge mozzarella.

Beer Forget about Guinness, in Cork a pint of 'the black stuff' is either Beamish or Murphy's.

Potato pie Wash down this local speciality from KC's (p129) with Tanora – a tangerine-flavoured 'mineral' (local slang for soda).

Must-try sandwich	Best cheese selection
O'Flynn's 'The Cork Boi' (p144)	Mahon Point (p147)

CONNECT & FIND YOUR WAY

Wi-fi Available everywhere, with free hotspots in libraries and public parks. If you're getting a SIM card, Vodafone has the best reception and has a store on Patrick's St in Cork city. Note there are some reception black spots in rural areas.

Navigation Google maps works well and everywhere is signposted. Friendly locals will always give directions.

WHERE TO STAY

Cork, especially the city, is expensive, with hotel accommodation averaging €120 a night. Hostels, B&Bs and Airbnbs are more affordable. Options book up fast during high season, festivals and bank holidays.

Place	Pro/Con
Cork City	Transport hub; widest selection of accommodation, tour operators, nightlife and restaurants.
Ballincollig	Near the city, connected by 24-hour bus; regional park with walking trails; historical gunpowder mills.
Kinsale	Start of the Wild Atlantic Way; colourful, historic town with great restaurants.
Clonakilty	Seaside town with beaches, friendly locals and DeBarra's for live music.
Skibbereen	Saturday market and historical, artistic vibes. Close to attractions.
Bantry	Friday market and stunning bay location. Explore Beara and Sheep's Head Peninsulas and Gougane Barra.

SAVE YOUR MONEY

Look for Pre-Theatre or Early Bird restaurant menus.
Tap water is potable and free.
Deli counters in shops like Centra have reasonably priced food.

MONEY

Taxis FREE NOW, similar to Uber, offers discounted rides (free-now.com/ie).

Leap Card A bus pass giving 30% discount on cash fares. Works on Cork buses and in other cities. Visitor cards available (leapcard.ie).

15 The Culinary **CAPITAL**

GASTRONOMY | MARKETS | DAY TRIPS

■■■■■ With the country's longest coastline and fertile farmlands, Cork has long been regarded as Ireland's culinary capital. It's home to a famous food market and cookery school, and more than 75% of the country's artisan producers are based in West Cork. All of this combines to make Cork gloriously gastronomic, packed with everything from casual cafes to fine-dining restaurants.

🔯 **How to**

Getting around Be sure to book a table, particularly for evening meals on weekends, bank holidays and during festivals, as popular places can book out fast.

Traditional delicacies Buttered eggs, crubeens (boiled, battered and fried pig's feet), drisheen (a blood sausage similar to black pudding) and tripe (the lining of a sheep or cow's stomach).

Top tip For maximum gluttonous comfort, loose-fitting clothing is advised.

Left The Bulman, Kinsale **Far left top** Cooking at the Ballymaloe Cookery School **Far left bottom** Carrageen moss

Cork's Best Food Experiences

Ballymaloe House Pioneering farm-to-table, Irish country-house cooking in the 1960s, generations of the Allen family continue a tradition of excellence with their slow-food philosophy. Opt to stay overnight or simply dine at Ballymaloe House. Keen cooks can take a course in the award-winning cookery school.

Skibbereen Farmers Market Every Saturday the historic West Cork town of Skibbereen bustles with its vibrant and colourful farmers market. The market attracts the area's best artisanal food and craft producers.

Secrets of seaweed For a unique sea vegetable experience, forage for seaweed with **Atlantic Sea Kayaking** (atlanticsea kayaking.com) in Skibbereen. On the 'Secrets of Seaweed' tour, at low tide, your guide will teach you how to identify the different types and how to pick them sustainably. You'll also learn about the culinary, cosmetic and medicinal uses of seaweed. Tip: try Carrageen Moss pudding in Cork. Can you guess the secret ingredient?

Kinsale scene Kinsale has a long-standing reputation as Ireland's gourmet town. With over 50 eateries, there's something for everyone. **Fishy Fishy, Man Friday** and **The Bulman** are firm favourites, but **Bastion** is where you'll find a Michelin Bib Gourmand. For cheap eats, try **Dino's** fresh fish and chips with mushy peas. Head to **Blacks of Kinsale** and choose from a unique range of craft beers and spirits to wash your meal down.

✂ Modern Delicacies

Chipper Unique to Cork, a local chip shop favourite is the humble potato pie. A ball of herby mashed potato is battered and deep-fried, with variations including cheese and/or onion. KC's in Douglas (be sure to try a filled pitta) and Jackie Lennox's on Bandon Rd are among the best chippers in the city. A battle wages on between locals over which is the best.

Boutique Cork coffee Cork coffee lovers sip on Badger & Dodo coffee. It's served in city cafes; there's a flagship in Fermoy and two cafes in Cork city, on Barrack St and South Mall.

16

The Wonderful
WILD WEST

OUTDOORS | ROAD TRIP | SCENERY

▬▬▬ Remote, untouched and inspiring, West Cork is an outdoor lover's dream. Visit picturesque villages, see a 3000-year-old stone circle and drive through dramatic landscapes that will leave you in awe, as you explore the jewel in Cork's crown.

 How to

Getting around Although there are public buses between towns, driving is always the best choice.

When to go Blue skies and calm weather are more likely from May to September.

Scenic stops Keep an eye out for lay-bys where you can pull over to get those wild landscape shots.

Driving tips Drive slowly as roads can be narrow and watch out for large farm vehicles and sheep on the roads.

Driving the Beara Peninsula

Many visitors to West Cork overlook the Beara Peninsula in favour of the better-known Ring of Kerry route. However, the Ring of Beara scenic drive offers just as much as its neighbour, if not more. It's a chance to get off the beaten track while navigating narrow *boreens* (country lanes), giving way to livestock and taking in some of the country's most breathtaking scenery, on the Beara Peninsula.

The isolated, unspoilt 128km headland drive begins in the quaint seaside town of **Glengarriff**. Head south to Adrigole, the jumping-off point for the inland **Healy Pass** drive, which ends at Lauragh Bridge in County Kerry. Enjoy the inspiring vistas as you continue to Castletownbere, where you can explore the ruins of **Dunboy Castle** nearby.

✖️ Taste of West Cork

Every September over 10 days, A Taste of West Cork Food Festival celebrates the culinary delights and home-grown produce of the region. With over 50 local towns and villages and nine islands represented, the festival is the ultimate introduction to local delicacies. It's an essential event for any foodie (atasteofwestcork.com).

Left Inchydoney Beach (p132) **Above left** Healy Pass **Above right** Eyeries (p132)

At the peninsula's end lies **Dursey Island**, a detour accessible by cable car. On a clear day, the stark **Skellig Islands** can often be seen, and sometimes dolphins. Driving back up the western side of the headland, stop for a swim at **Ballydonegan Beach** before visiting three picture-postcard Irish villages – Allihies, Eyeries and Ardgroom – where many resident **artists' homes** double as galleries. You can also tour the **Copper Mine Museum** at Allihies, the most westerly copper mine in Europe.

Further up the coast, you cross the border into Kerry just after Cappacloghernane. The views of **Kenmare Bay** on this stretch are magnificent. Continue until you connect with the N71. Hang a right and make your way back to Glengarriff, crossing back into Cork via Turners Rock Tunnel and the striking Caha Pass.

Best of the West

Beautifully untamed and unapologetically gorgeous, **Mizen Head** marks the most

🛶 West Cork Adventures

Night kayaking trips can be arranged with **Atlantic Sea Kayaking** (atlanticsea kayaking.com) on Lough Hyne, Ireland's only salt-water lake and the country's first Marine Nature Reserve.

Inchydoney Beach is popular with surfers, offering multiple peaks on either side of the headland. Rentals are available from **Inchydoney Surf School** (inchydoney surfschool.com).

Walk some of the 250km of trails on Sheep's Head, birdwatch along the Seven Heads Walk in Courtmacsherry, or hike one of six trails in **Gougane Barra Forest Park**.

Kayak amid a 40-strong colony of seals in the calm, sheltered waters of Adrigole harbour on a trip with Wild Atlantic Wildlife (wildatlanticwildlife.ie).

Left Gougane Barra Forest Park
Below Drombeg Stone Circle

southwesterly point on the island of Ireland. Crossing the bridge to the signal tower, keep an eye out for seals in the gorge far below and look for whales and dolphins swimming offshore. There's also a small visitor centre and cafe.

Hugging the rugged coastline for 70km, the **Sheep's Head Peninsula drive** is dramatic and awe-inspiring. Completely untouched and undeveloped, this little remote corner of West Cork will give you that off-the-beaten-track feeling you have been searching for. Embrace the isolation and enjoy the peace and quiet.

Located on the wild Beara Peninsula, the **Healy Pass** takes you along winding, bending narrow roads that snake through this mountainous landscape and over the Caha Mountains. Beginning at Adrigole Bridge in Cork and ending 12km over the road in Lauragh Bridge, County Kerry, the views are quite simply spectacular.

A short drive from Glandore is **Drombeg Stone Circle**, an archaeological treasure. This 3000-year-old site consists of 17 standing stones. The stones form a distinct circle, measuring 9.3m in diameter and orientated so the sun's rays illuminate the flat axial stone facing the entrance on the Winter Solstice.

17

Castles & Stately
HOMES

CASTLES | HISTORY | GARDENS

Rural castles and coastal homes with impeccably manicured gardens speckle the rolling Cork countryside. Cork Harbour, the second-largest natural harbour in the world, was frequently Ireland's first line of defence from invaders. Impressive medieval strongholds and fortifications stood the test of time.

How to

Getting around While Blackrock Castle is easily accessible from Cork city and Kinsale is connected by bus, car is the best way to visit castles and stately homes further afield.

When to go Although the best weather is June to August, the gardens come to life with colour in spring and autumn.

Irish gifts Family-run Blarney Woollen Mills offers a huge selection of Irish-made crafts, products and souvenirs.

Marvellous Medieval Castles

Blackrock Castle A stone's throw from Cork city centre, this picture-perfect castle could be straight out of a fairy tale. Restored as a functional observatory, it has a popular cafe on-site with expansive views across the Lee. Guided tours are available along with planetarium shows and interactive exhibits.

Blarney Castle Cork's – maybe Ireland's – most famous castle is a must. Be sure to kiss the Blarney Stone for the 'gift of the gab'. Acrophobics beware: to kiss the stone, first you climb 127 steps to the castle top, you then lay down, hold on to iron bars and lower your head backwards from a ledge. An attendant assists. Years ago, visitors were held by the ankles and lowered head first. Queues can be over an hour long in summer.

⚠ Cork's 9/11 Memorial

Just outside Kinsale is the Ringfinnan Garden of Remembrance, containing 343 trees – each one dedicated to a firefighter, plus one for their chaplain, who died on 11 September 2001. The garden was established by local nurse Kathleen Murphy, who lived in New York for over 30 years and is also memorialised in the garden.

Left Blackrock Castle **Above left** Bantry House & Garden (p137) **Above right** Charles Fort (p136)

Charles Fort Just outside Kinsale, Charles Fort is a fantastically preserved star-shaped fortress looming over the harbour. Dating back to the 17th century, it features gun bastions used to defend Ireland against Spanish and French fleets and was still in military use until 1922. There's a visitor's centre onsite with guided tours available.

Dunlough Castle The crumbling ruins of Dunlough Castle are on the Mizen Head Peninsula, at a point named 'Three Castle Head' because of the three towers that still stand. One of the oldest Norman castles in southern Ireland, it's only accessible by foot and is shrouded in legends and ghost stories. There's accommodation nearby (threecastle head.ie).

Magnificent Houses, Glorious Gardens

Fota Island Fota House and its magnificent 19th-century decor offer a unique insight into

🏛 Floating Garden

Hidden in the hills of Skibbereen's Liss Ard Estate is the **Irish Sky Garden**. Designed by American artist James Turrell, this interactive art installation takes inspiration from Celtic, Egyptian and Mayan archaeological concepts. Visitors enter via a stone archway, through a long megalithic-like passage, and up steps that lead to a grass-lined crater. In the centre is a large stone slab where you lie back and look up to experience the sky framed by the rim of the crater. Turrell says: 'The most important thing is that inside turns into outside and the other way around.'

Left Dunlough Castle
Below Blarney Castle (p135)

the past. Art lovers take note, Fota House has one of the finest collections of landscape painting outside the National Gallery of Ireland. Fota Arboretum & Gardens spans 27 acres and features restored Victorian glasshouses. Child-friendly activities make it a firm favourite with Cork families. The house shares a car park (€3 all day) with Fota Wildlife Park, so it's convenient to visit both on the same trip. Fota Island Resort offers luxury accommodation and golf.

Bantry House & Garden The incredible location of Bantry House right on Bantry Bay affords it sweeping views of the water and Caha Mountains. The garden features seven terraces, a fountain, a large wisteria circle and 100 steps leading to a woodland. The estate has rested with the same family since the 1700s and contains original furnishings and artefacts.

Doneraile Court Eighteenth-century Doneraile Court is an outstanding example of Georgian architecture, towering majestically over a 160-hectare landscaped parkland and wildlife estate. Visitors can enjoy beautiful water features, several pathways and graded walks. Keep your eyes peeled: if you're lucky you might spot some of the various deer and Kerry cattle that call the estate home.

18

Islands &
BEACHES

**EXPLORATION | OUTDOORS |
WILD ATLANTIC WAY**

West Cork is home to some of the most spectacular coastline in the country. Spend time exploring the unique islands scattered off the coast, go whale-watching, or find your own slice of paradise on one of the county's sensational beaches.

🗺 How to

Getting around As more rural parts of West Cork can be quite isolated, it's wise to top up your fuel when you can.

When to go Check the forecast before you travel, as ferry and cable car crossings can be cancelled in bad weather.

Camping Wild camping is not technically legal but it is tolerated in places. Be respectful and leave no trace. There are also plenty of campsites around the county.

CORK EXPERIENCES

Island Life

Bere Island For windswept scenery, you won't get much better than Bere Island. Visitors can expect sandy beaches, ring forts, quiet coves and magnificent views of the Slieve Miskish and Caha Mountains back on the mainland. There is also an 1899 military fortification to visit.

Cape Clear Precariously positioned on the edge of the continental shelf, Cape Clear is one of Europe's premier whale- and dolphin-watching locations. Venture out and explore its natural beauty on foot, or seek out one of the cosy pubs on the island and practice your Irish language skills with the friendly locals, who call their home Oileán Chléire.

🍺 Coastal Craic

Whether you sip on a stout with a view at O'Sullivan's in Crookhaven, step back in time at Levi's in Ballydehob or Ma Murphy's in Bantry, or enjoy the music sessions at De Barra's in Clonakilty, having the craic in one of West Cork's favourite seaside watering holes is an absolute necessity.

Left Cable car to Dursey Island **Above left** Barleycove Beach (p141) **Above right** Seals, Garnish Island (p140)

Dursey Island Ireland's only cable car connects Dursey Island with the mainland. Carrying a maximum of six people at a time, the eight-minute trip transports you 250m above the ocean. The island itself is a traffic-free offshore oasis with a raw, rugged landscape.

Sherkin Island Known as the island of the arts, Sherkin Island is home to a creative community of artists, whose work is sold in nearby Baltimore. Countless hidden coves and beaches punctuate the coastline making it the perfect location for any nature, wildlife or outdoors enthusiast to explore.

Garnish Island Sheltered by Bantry Bay, Garnish Island has an almost subtropical climate and is home to a series of vibrant gardens where tropical plants from all over the world grow. Keep an eye out for seals that are often found basking on the island's shores.

🐋 Beautiful Baltimore

Baltimore is the epicentre of West Cork's **whale-watching** scene. Depending on the season, you can see minke whales, harbour porpoise, common dolphins, humpback and fin whales, basking sharks and even the odd leatherback turtle. A tour of this special marine area makes for a truly memorable experience; book with Baltimore Sea Safari (baltimoresea safari.ie) or Whale Watch West Cork (whalewatch westcork.com).

Standing 15.2m tall, the cone-shaped **Baltimore Beacon** is a signal tower marking the headland at the narrow strait between Sherkin and the harbour. It's known locally as 'Lot's Wife', after a biblical figure that solidified into a pillar of salt. Visitors to this odd structure are guaranteed unbeatable coastal views.

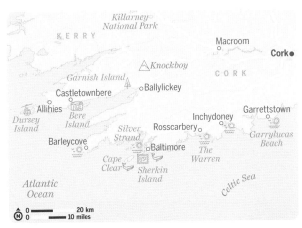

Left Baltimore Beacon **Below** Sherkin Island

Sun, Sea & Sand

Garrylucas Beach A short drive from Cork foodie capital Kinsale, Garrylucas is a long inviting stretch of sand with small dunes to the eastern end. Just up the road is the famous Old Head Of Kinsale headland, with tall cliffs harbouring native birds and other wildlife, as well as a golf course, making this is a popular beach with tourists and locals alike.

Inchydoney A popular surfing beach, Inchydoney is an expansive Blue Flag strip that beckons beach-goers. Explore the expansive dunes, ride the waves or enjoy a picnic on the peaceful sands of this Cork favourite.

The Warren Nestled away down a quiet road at the mouth of Roscarberry River, The Warren is a small, secluded beach that can attract big crowds in the summer. It's a beautiful location, listed as a Natural Heritage Area.

Barleycove Beach Surrounded by an endless sea of green fields on all sides, the white sands of Barleycove Beach are instantly recognisable on approach. This truly is one of the most breathtaking beaches in the country.

Silver Strand To find your West Cork beach island paradise, head for this stunning strand on Sherkin Island. Away from the crowds, you can enjoy the clear waters and sun-kissed sands of this beautiful beach in peace and quiet.

19 Stroll Through
CORK CITY

WALKING | HISTORY | CULTURE

▬▬▬▬ Cork's compact size makes it perfect for on-foot exploration. Learn about the world's largest butter market, explore University College Cork's charming campus and experience amazing views of the city from an old church tower with this self-guided walking tour.

TRISH PUNCH/EYEEM/500PX/GETTY IMAGES ©

🗺 How to

Getting around The start of the walk, St Fin Barre's Cathedral, is a 10-minute walk from Cork city centre.

When to go Start the walk at 9.30am to catch the first cathedral tour and then have the whole day to explore the route.

How long Set aside one to two hours for this walk (more if you want to linger along the route); the total distance is around 5km.

Celebrate Play 'Happy Birthday' on the Shandon Bells if it's your special day.

🏞 Picnic at Fitzgerald's Park

After University College Cork, take a break at every Corkonian's favourite green space, Fitzgerald's Park, with a peaceful picnic along the banks of the Lee. Look for Daly's bridge (pictured left), a pedestrian suspension bridge at the park's northern end, locally known as 'Shaky Bridge'. Walk across and you'll soon see how it got its nickname.

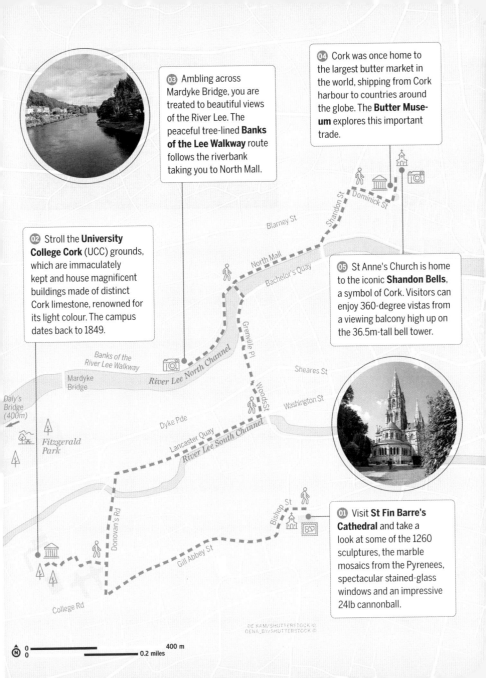

03 Ambling across Mardyke Bridge, you are treated to beautiful views of the River Lee. The peaceful tree-lined **Banks of the Lee Walkway** route follows the riverbank taking you to North Mall.

04 Cork was once home to the largest butter market in the world, shipping from Cork harbour to countries around the globe. The **Butter Museum** explores this important trade.

02 Stroll the **University College Cork** (UCC) grounds, which are immaculately kept and house magnificent buildings made of distinct Cork limestone, renowned for its light colour. The campus dates back to 1849.

05 St Anne's Church is home to the iconic **Shandon Bells**, a symbol of Cork. Visitors can enjoy 360-degree vistas from a viewing balcony high up on the 36.5m-tall bell tower.

01 Visit **St Fin Barre's Cathedral** and take a look at some of the 1260 sculptures, the marble mosaics from the Pyrenees, spectacular stained-glass windows and an impressive 24lb cannonball.

Blarney St

Shandon St

Dominick St

North Mall

Bachelor's Quay

Grenville Pl

Sheares St

Banks of the River Lee Walkway

River Lee North Channel

Mardyke Bridge

Woods St

Washington St

Daly's Bridge (400m)

Fitzgerald Park

Dyke Pde

Lancaster Quay

River Lee South Channel

Donovan's Rd

Bishop St

Gill Abbey St

College Rd

0 — 400 m
0 — 0.2 miles
(N)

Charting the English Market

FEEDING CORK FOR OVER 200 YEARS

Trading in Cork's city centre since the 18th century, the English Market is so much more than a place of commerce. It has endured famine, fires, floods, wars, multiple recessions and two proposed demolitions. The market is a social hub and a slice of, as the locals say, 'pure' Cork.

Left Olive stand, English Market
Middle Stained-glass ceiling, English
Market **Right** Chocolate pralines

© NIBLERO/SHUTTERSTOCK ©

Development

The economic development of Cork in the 18th century saw the reclamation of the marshes. The city's Irish language name, 'Corcaigh', meaning 'marsh', derives from the fact that Cork's main streets were once waterways running between islands, which were reclaimed and built over, creating the city's present layout.

In the 1780s, inspired by the development of covered markets in England, Cork's corporation proposed developing a covered food market in the heart of this reclaimed centre. Foundations were laid on Grand Parade in 1786 and the Grand Parade Meat Market opened the summer construction was completed, in 1788.

Expansion

Taking shape gradually over the following years, fish, poultry and vegetable markets were soon added. But it wasn't until 19 December 1862 that Princes Street Market was formalised with a roof. This was also when the ornamental frontage, entrance and balcony area (doubling the number of stalls) came in.

The Grand Parade entrance was officially opened on 14 July 1881. The clock came next, which still stands at the centre of the facade, with the Cork coat of arms positioned above.

Setbacks

During the War of Independence, in 1920, British soldiers looted and burned buildings in Cork. Fire spread from a nearby store and the roof of the Princes Street Market was

extensively damaged. Miraculously, though, this was the only scarring that the English Market suffered at the time.

Much greater damage was wrought in 1980, when a fire caused by a gas explosion on 19 June ravaged the English Market. Princes Street Market was destroyed, except for its fountain, which escaped with minor damage. Luckily, Grand Parade Market came through unscathed.

Modern Marketplace

The English Market is Ireland's oldest covered market and...the heartbeat of Cork's city centre.

Princes Street Market was fully restored by October 1981, receiving a gold medal from Europa Nostra in 1983 for its enhancement of Europe's architectural heritage. The overall space remains but features a circular arrangement using the refurbished fountain as a focal point. The upstairs gallery includes a cafe area and new trading space.

Alongside the usual offerings of fish, meat, fruit and veg, foodies will delight in the array of exotic cheeses and olives, cured meats, foreign cuisine specialists and imported herbs and spices on offer at the deli counters in the centre of the market. More adventurous appetites can sample traditional Irish delicacies, such as old-school favourites of crubeens, drisheen and tripe. The English Market is Ireland's oldest covered market and even after more than 200 years of service, it remains not just a gastronomic retail experience but also the heartbeat of Cork's city centre.

✅ Why an 'English' Market?

The market was originally established by Cork's Protestant corporation when Ireland was under British rule. In 1840, local governments were reformed and a Catholic majority took power in Cork. They set up another covered food market, St Peter's, now the Bodega Bar on Cornmarket Street. This became known as the 'Irish Market' to differentiate it from its older counterpart, the 'English Market', which was associated with its Protestant founders. At the time, less well-off, working-class Corkonians shopped in St Peter's Market where food prices were lower and the English Market catered to Cork's wealthier, more affluent residents.

Listings

BEST OF THE REST

 ### Coffee Culture

Alchemy Coffee & Bookstore

Hidden away on Cork's Barrack St, this rustic cafe decorated with old and new books is the perfect spot for a coffee break. There's a choice of brewing methods for filter coffee lovers.

Filter Espresso & Brew Bar

On George's Quay in the city centre, this bright riverside coffee shop serves some of the city's best coffee. Choose from a variety of brewing methods and blends while admiring the posters and coffee gadgets.

 ### Local Produce Champions

Paradiso €€€

On Lancaster Quay, this award-winning vegetarian restaurant is a Cork city institution. With a focus on contemporary cuisine and locally sourced, seasonal ingredients, it's guaranteed to satisfy even the hardiest carnivore.

Farmgate Café €€

Upstairs in the English Market, this cafe sources its ingredients directly from the vendors below. Sample local delicacies, great coffee and gluten-free treats while watching the hustle and bustle. Check out 'The Great Wall of Cork' – a unique collection of poems by Cork Irish and international poets, framed and on display.

Quay Co-op €

Located on Sullivan's Quay in the city centre, this whole-food organic restaurant and deli utilises local produce to create vegetarian and vegan versions of local favourites. There's a great food store on-site for self-caterers, with additional locations in Carrigaline and Ballincollig.

 ### Unique City Eats

Iyer's €

For a taste of southern India in southern Ireland, this teeny family-run vegetarian cafe serves the best masala dosa this side of Mysuru. Delicious desserts and coffee too. Located on Pope's Quay. Cash only.

Ichigo Ichie €€€

Cork's only Michelin-star chef, Takasahi Miyazaki has combined Japanese technique and Irish ingredients with mouth-watering results. The Sheares St venue serves sushi and kaiseki ryori – a multi-course Japanese meal.

Miyazaki €€

For a more affordable taste of Japan, check out chef Takasahi Miyazaki's takeaway branch on Evergreen St, featuring curries, noodles and rice bowls.

 ### Craft Beer & Spirits

Jameson Distillery Midleton

Head east to Midleton for a behind-the-scenes glimpse at how 'uisce beatha', the water of life, is made. Tour the distillery, taste rare whiskey or immerse yourself in a full-day whiskey academy experience.

Franciscan Well Bar & Brewery

The Fran has been brewing craft beers in the walls of an old Franciscan monastery in Cork since before it was trendy. Enjoy an additive-free, vegan-friendly pint of locally named brews like Blarney Blonde, Rebel Red and Shandon Stout. Sip your pint in the beer garden or enjoy a craft cocktail in the Monk Bar, and snack on pizza.

Longueville House Distillery

Head north just outside Mallow to tour what was Ireland's first micro-distillery, established in 1985 in a listed Georgian country house. Afterwards, sample the award-winning apple cider and apple brandy.

Kinsale Mead Company

Learn about mead, the world's oldest alcoholic drink made from honey, at this award-winning family-run meadery. Founded in 2016, it's the first in Ireland in 200 years.

 ## Day Trips

Gougane Barra

A lush forest park in Múscarí, the Cork Gaeltacht area, spanning more than 339 acres at the foot of the Sheehy Mountains. Within it, there's a lake with a tiny island housing a picturesque church named after St Finbarr, the patron saint of Cork.

 ## Fun Festivals

Guinness Cork Jazz Festival

Get your dancing shoes on for this toe-tapping Cork music festival. Held in venues across the city every October bank holiday weekend, it's been attracting jazz fans and musicians to the banks of the Lee since 1978.

Cork Midsummer Festival

This 16-day multidisciplinary festival held every June features performers from all around the world. Theatre, street performances, dance, visual art installations and circus acts combine to bring the city to life.

Kinsale Gourmet Festival

Foodies, prepare to feast. Running for more than 45 years in Kinsale, this annual foodie festival hosts Mad Hatter tea parties and walking food tours every October.

Jameson Distillery, Midleton

 ## Farmers Markets

Midleton Farmers Market

Established by local farmers and Darina Allen of Ballymaloe cooking school, this lively market is held every Saturday. It's one of the oldest and most varied markets in Ireland. The Ballymaloe Cookery Stall is a favourite.

Mahon Point Farmers Market

Cork's largest farmers market is hosted by Mahon Point Shopping Centre every Thursday morning, usually accompanied by live music. Head to Gubbeen Smokehouse for award-winning cheeses.

Bantry Farmers Market

From early morning to early afternoon every Friday in Bantry's Wolfe Tone Sq. As well as food, there's crafts here and an array of bric-a-brac and antiques stalls. The first Friday of every month is a traditional Fair Day.

Scan for things to see, do and try in Cork

KERRY

HIKING | SCENIC | BEACHES

Experience Kerry online

Hiker, Slea Head

KERRY
Trip Builder

With pristine beaches, a rich history and exhilarating driving routes, it's no wonder Kerry is known as 'The Kingdom'. Discover what makes it so special and plan an unforgettable trip including the vibrant Kerry Gaeltacht, one of Ireland's Irish-speaking strongholds.

Enjoy a refreshing seaweed bath in **Ballybunion** (p159)
🕓 ½ day

Drive around gorgeous **Slea Head** and experience Gaeltacht hospitality (p152)
🕓 1-2 days

Don hiking boots and trek the beautiful **Kerry Camino** (p156)
🕓 2-3 days

Have a satisfying pint (or two) in the cosy pubs of **Dingle** (p164)
🕓 ½ day

Explore **Valentia Island** and climb **Geokaun Mountain** for panoramic views (p160)
🕓 1 day

Boat over to monastic **Skellig Michael** for *Star Wars* fandom (p168)
🕓 1 day

Explore bookable experiences in Kerry online

Atlantic Ocean

CLARE

Shannon Estuary

Cashen Bay

Brandon Bay

Tralee Bay

Tralee

Camp

Slieve Mish Mountains

Dingle Peninsula

Blasket Islands

Dingle Bay

KERRY

Kells

Cahersiveen

Chapeltown

Iveragh Peninsula

Ballinskelligs

Skellig Islands

Scariff Island

Kenmare River

Dursey Island

CORK

Sheep's Head

Mizen Head

Celtic Sea

N 0 — 20 km
0 — 10 miles

Practicalities

ARRIVING

Kerry Airport Car hire and taxis here. A 20-minute walk to Farranfore Station, for trains to Tralee and Killarney.

Casement Train Station Tralee's main station. Bus Éireann on-site for rural routes.

FIND YOUR WAY

Local tourist offices in hubs such as Killarney and Tralee will have guides, tips and maps. Enquire about other seasonal offices.

MONEY

Cards are commonly accepted in Kerry, but cash is handy for parking metres if you're stopping in towns.

WHERE TO STAY

Place	Pro/Con
Dingle	Popular hub in West Kerry Gaeltacht; hiking, beaches, rich heritage. Tourist hotspot.
Killarney	Hotels and guesthouses galore. Best for families and nights out; expect summer crowds.
Kenmare	Great base for foodies and south Kerry exploration. Public transport access poor.
Portmagee	Quiet seaside village with access to famous islands. Limited accommodation.

EATING & DRINKING

Dingle Gin ice cream Not to be missed at Murphy's ice-cream parlour (murphysicecream.ie).

Micilín Muc black pudding Award-winning producer of traditional blood puddings. Found in shops across Kerry.

Cromane mussels Super meaty shellfish from the pure waters of Castlemaine Harbour.

Must-try tapas Sol y Sombra (p174)

Best for whiskey & music Dick Mack's live music nights (p167)

GETTING AROUND

Car Driving is the best way to reach Kerry's more remote locations and rural villages.

Train The main towns of Kerry, such as Killarney, are connected by rail.

Tour bus A popular option with groups, particularly around the Ring of Kerry.

 JAN - MAR Brisk. Perfect for active days out to warm up.

 APR - JUN Brighter, warmer days. Popular touring season.

JUL - SEP Warm to hot, with settled beach weather.

 OCT - DEC Cold and often wet. Ideal for retreats by the fire.

20

Slea Head Drive
SCENERY

TOURING | COASTLINE | DAY TRIP

▬▬▬ Spend the day traversing one of the most spectacular driving routes in Ireland. This circular tour takes you along clifftop roads and through the heart of the West Kerry Irish speaking region, Corca Dhuibhne, with the thundering Atlantic Ocean by your side.

How to

Getting around The best way to experience this route is by car, but people also hike and cycle it. Rent from Dingle Bikes (dinglebikes.com).

When to go Although open year-round, summer is best to enjoy a splash in the sea.

Top tips Start in Dingle and travel the Slea Head Drive clockwise. This is the recommended route as you will be able to avoid meeting larger tour buses head-on.

Incredible Views

Around the southern end of the drive is a large white crucifix with some exceptional views of the Atlantic. In summer this is one of the most congested parts of the route; an alternative lookout spot is **Dunmore Head**, where a short hike offers views of the Blasket Islands sitting proudly in the ocean.

Framed by cliffs, pause to admire the dramatic top-down view of the winding stone pier at **Dunquin** before descending to catch the ferry to Great Blasket Island. This picture-perfect place has made many a postcard – just don't drive down to it or you may end up stuck. While there is no car park, you can park along the roadside and walk down the winding routeway.

The Gaeltacht Experience

Corca Dhuibhne (Dingle Peninsula) is West Kerry's Irish-speaking region and locals will appreciate it if you make an effort to understand how the communities use the language in their everyday lives. Learn a few words or phrases and consider taking Dublin City University's **free Irish courses** online. See futurelearn.com/partners/dcu.

Left Dunquin **Above left** View between Slea Head and Dunmore Head **Above right** Great Blasket Island

Clogher Beach has an even better view of the impressive 'Sleeping Giant', as Great Blasket Island is colloquially known, laying at peace in the ocean.

Historical Sites

West Kerry is steeped in history and there are countless sites along the Slea Head Drive. A good place to get an intimate look at the history and culture of the Gaeltacht is at **Músaem Chorca Dhuibhne** in Baile an Fheirtéaraigh (Ballyferriter). Other places of note are **Cashel Murphy**, an early Celtic settlement overlooking Dingle Bay, and **Eask Tower**, a striking solid stone building, which was built in 1847 to guide the ships into the harbour.

One of the most important historical sites on this driving route is **Cill Mhaoilcéadair** (Kilmalkeder), where a certain stillness lingers over the grass-lined pebbles. This early Medieval Christian site is just 8km from Dingle,

🔭 Baile na nGall's Best Experiences

An exhilarating dip At high tide, jump off the second slip into the pristine Atlantic with Mt Brandon and Cruach Mhárthainn as your backdrop.

Unspoilt vistas Views of the Three Sisters are picture-perfect at dusk, as the sun dips behind Binn Dhiarmada.

Traditional racing The Regatta usually takes place on early June weekends. Locals compete in a traditional boat called a *naomhóg*.

A creamy pint Relax at Tigh Bheaglaoich. Enjoy fresh fish and chips overlooking Tráigh an Chléirigh. The ocean spray will meet your lips.

Recommended by Sláine Ní Chathalláin, broadcaster with RTÉ Raidió na Gaeltachta @SlaineNi

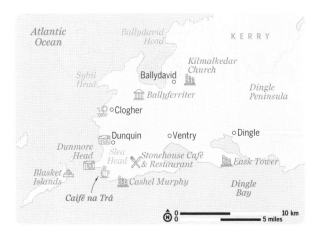

Left Baile na nGall pier **Below** Stonehouse Café & Restaurant

yet rarely crowded. Estimated to have been built in the 7th century, the existing remains are spread over 10 acres. Highlights include a 1.2m-high Latin alphabet stone and *bullán* stones (used to collect water). A T-shaped cross – or *tau* – has been described by the Office of Public Works (OPW) as a sundial. However, some historians think it was more likely a 'scratch dial', used to indicate the times of religious service.

At the back wall of the Romanesque church, visitors can attempt to go through Cró na Snáthaide (eye of the needle). If you can make it to the other side, it's said to be a sure sign that you will get into heaven. From the graveyard, there are breathtaking views of Smerwick Harbour and beyond.

Scenic Food Stops

The **Stonehouse Café & Restaurant**, just a 10-minute spin west from Ventry, is a favourite for those on the Slea Head Drive and has outdoor dining that looks across to Valentia Island on the Iveragh Peninsula. The ocean views are complemented by the restaurant's speciality: seafood.

Further northwest, the popular **Caifé na Trá** near Coumeenole beach also has outdoor space and views of Great Blasket Island. Tuck into soup and toasties – best enjoyed with freshly ground coffee.

21 Walking the CAMINO

HISTORY | HIKING | BEACHES

Follow in the footsteps of St Brendan, traversing open mountainsides, through woodland and over river crossings. Stacks of cut turf dot the landscape along the path, which traces small roads and country trails from Tralee to Dingle. All you need is three days.

🗺 How to

Getting around A day's walk can take five to seven hours. Discuss bag transfers and the return trip to Tralee with kerrycamino.com, or get the local Bus Éireann back to Tralee from The Tracks in Dingle.

When to go Try autumn, or join the annual group walk on the May Bank Holiday weekend.

Top tip Visit the serene Minard Castle (pictured above) in Kilmurray, on the edge of the water with views of the Iveragh Peninsula.

☀ Don't Miss
Inch Strand

Detour onto the beach. Walkers often pass by here around lunchtime on the third day of their hike. It's an impressive strand of windswept sand dunes, with Rossbeigh Beach, the Iveragh Peninsula and Slieve Mish Mountains in the background.

Recommended by
Ingrid Boyle and Mike O'Donnell of the Kerry Camino committee
@TheKerryCamino

03 Go back in time with historical memorabilia at **The Railway Tavern** (known locally as Mike Nail's) in Camp and learn about Kerry's railroads in this cosy, quaint pub.

01 Detour at Blennerville Windmill and take the peaceful, grassy path to **Slí na n-Éan** right by the water's edge. It has great views of Tralee Bay at sunset.

05 See the **Lispole Viaduct** (built in the 1890s) and learn about the importance and history of the railway line in Kerry through information panels in this small Gaeltacht village.

Atlantic Ocean

Tralee Bay

Tralee KERRY

Blennerville

Camp

Slieve Mish Mountains

Sybil Head

Dingle Peninsula

Lougher

Inch

Dingle

Annascaul

Slea Head

Inch Point

Dingle Bay

Glenbeigh

Iveragh Peninsula

Killarney

Lough Leane

Killarney National Park

02 Visit the ruined famine village of **Killelton**, overgrown with shrubbery. Its inhabitants were evicted and the area abandoned in the 19th century; today it's a poignant reminder of the past.

04 Named after the Irish Antarctic explorer Tom Crean, **The South Pole Inn** in Annascaul has treasured memories from his adventures and serves up great food and drink.

Ⓝ 0 ___ 20 km
0 ___ 10 miles

22 Beaches &
ISLANDS

BEACHES | ISLANDS | RELAXATION

Often empty with rarely a crowd in sight, one of the greatest things about Kerry is its beaches with crystal-clear waters and islands swimming in historical significance.

How to

Getting around Hire a car or bike to get the most out of the Irish countryside. If you've more time to spare, consider hiking too.

When to go Summer has the best weather, but this is exactly when tour buses are in Kerry. Early summer (May) is particularly lovely.

Top tips Avoid public holidays. If planning to visit the Skelligs, it's necessary to book months in advance.

Peace & Quiet

Kerry beaches are far from crowded. Walk along the sandy **Baile an Sceilg** beach with Ballinskelligs Castle in the background, or spend the day relaxing at the secluded **Kells Bay** and harbour. **Wine Strand** is another remote beach tucked away in the West Kerry Gaeltacht, or head to glorious **Béal Bán**; its soft white sand makes it a family favourite. Parking is tight so get there early.

Surfers' Paradise

Hit the waves at **Ballybunion**, ease the muscles at Collin's Seaweed Baths, then head to **The Maharees** in Castlegregory to catch a surf break. **Banna Beach**, 13km from Tralee, is another local favourite for surfers and water sports enthusiasts.

Famous Writers

Three Great Blasket Islanders – Tomás Ó Criomhthain, Muiris Ó Súilleabháin and Peig Sayers – rose to fame through their books, which gave a true insight into island life and the harsh realities of living in such isolated conditions. Visit the **Blasket Centre** (blasket.ie) for more information.

Left Wine Strand **Above left** Banna Beach
Above right Great Blasket Island (p160)

Enchanting Islands

Take the ferry from Dunquin pier and spend the day on **Great Blasket Island**. Go back in time and see the islanders' former homes and relax on the beach. The local colony of seals love sprawling on the sand.

While Skellig Michael (p168) gets more favourable attention from tourists and movie fans, **Little Skellig** is fascinating too. The smaller of the famous pair, this island's astonishing bird haven is home to one of the largest colonies of gannets in the world.

Away from the coast, take a boat trip to **Innisfallen Island** in Lough Leane, starting from Ross Castle in Killarney. Innisfallen is the lake's largest island and contains the remains of an Augustinian priory as well as a small Romanesque church.

Chilled Beach Vibes

Unwind and make a splash in the ocean at **Derrynane Beach** off the Ring of Kerry. This clean

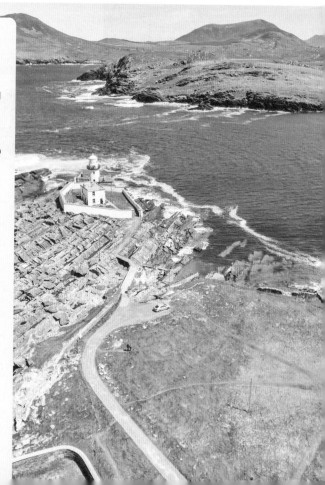

🗼 Valentia Island's Top Experiences

Skellig views Climb Bray Head and take the Loop Walk accompanied by local sheep. At the summit is a historic Martello Tower.

Historical Knightstown Famous for its King Scallop Festival in the summer, buildings here echo British design.

Picturesque lighthouse Picnic by the 17th-century lighthouse at Cromwell Point with the sound of crashing waves.

Geokaun Mountain Take the challenging climb to Valentia's highest point for unbeatable views.

Gorgeous grotto Visit the Virgin Mary and St Bernadette statues in the Valentia Slate Quarry, complete with waterfall.

Recommended by Séaghan Ó Súilleabháin, Kerryman and TikToker at Kerry Cowboy @Suilleabhanach

stretch of sand with rocky outcrops is much loved by locals in Caherdaniel. Derrynane has a natural harbour and is seldom busy. Walkers and swimmers embrace these Atlantic shores and families will love relaxing on the beach and exploring the rock pools. Lifeguards are on duty during the bathing season (June to August).

The inviting crystal-clear waters of Derrynane and fine soft sand are heavenly for those looking for a chilled day out. Top it off with pub grub and a fresh pint at **Keating's Bar** at the harbour. If you're lucky enough to time your visit with one of their evenings of music and song, you're in for a treat.

If the beach isn't enough for you, pass over a nearby sandy spit of land to reach **Abbey Island** and visit the ruins of St Finian's 8th-century abbey.

Just a short 10-minute stroll from the beach is **Derrynane House**, the impressive ancestral home of Daniel O'Connell. O'Connell, a lawyer, politician and subsequent statesman, is regarded as one of the greatest figures in Irish history.

KERRY EXPERIENCES

Left Valentia Island Lighthouse **Right** Derrynane House

23 Celebrations
OF OLD

CULTURE | NATURAL BEAUTY | FESTIVALS

With Kerry's deep Celtic roots, it's little surprise many of the region's communities still celebrate the ancient Celtic festivals: Imbolc for spring, Bealtaine for summer, Lughnasa in autumn for harvest, Samhain (Halloween) and the solstices in-between. From mountain pilgrimages to nights of feasting and music, these traditions are wonderful celebrations of life.

🗺 How to

Getting here/around
Killorglin is the largest festival hub and it has bus links with the nearby major towns of Killarney and Tralee, both accessible by rail and bus from Dublin. Use Local Link Kerry (locallink kerry.ie) for smaller village celebrations.

When to go The start of spring and autumn were vitally important events in the pagan calendar so it's no surprise that the best festivals are held at these times.

Top tip Book accommodation well in advance as the towns quickly fill up with festival-goers.

DONAVAN VOSIFOVI/ALAMY STOCK PHOTO ©

Left Puck Fair **Far left top** Biddy's Day parade, Killorglin **Far left bottom** King Puck statue, Killorglin

Biddy's Day The start of spring, Imbolc, is known today as St Brigid's Day or Biddy's Day. The townland of **Kilgobnet** has kept the old traditions of Biddy's Day (facebook.com/biddysday) alive for hundreds of years. 'Biddy Groups' dressed in white and handmade straw hats carry an effigy of Brigid (a Brídeóg) to every home to protect the community from evil spirits. It's on the Saturday closest to 1 February.

In the nearby town of **Killorglin** it has been expanded into a festival to include traditional music, dancing, storytelling and straw hat and Brídeóg workshops. In the evening, join the firelight procession through the town to see the crowning of the King of the Biddies.

Harvest Festival The village of **Cloghane** hosts a fantastic **Féile Lughnasa** (facebook.com/feilelughnasa) with a weekend of great music, storytelling and a unique parade where locals parody current events with satirical floats and costumes. In nearby **Brandon**, the blessing of the boats takes place by the pier. Join the ancient pilgrimage to **Mt Brandon** with knowledgeable locals, a ritual that's thousands of years old. Lughnasa celebrations are held on the last Sunday of July (the closest date to the traditional Celtic start of autumn).

The Goat King 'Ireland's oldest festival', **Puck Fair** (puckfair. ie), is the pride of Killorglin. While revellers feast, dance and sing for three days every August, 'King Puck', a wild goat, is crowned and placed on a pedestal. The festival's roots are grounded in Lughnasa (harvest festival), but its meaning is still debated. The town is filled with food stalls, street acts, music sessions and partying.

⚜ Celtic Connection

Significant days of the year were supplanted with Christian calendar dates in an effort to gain a foothold in the hearts and minds of the pagan people of Ireland. This resulted in a blending of ancient Celtic and early Christian practices.

Lughnasa, the harvest festival, marked the coming of autumn with bountiful feasts and pilgrimages to the top of sacred mountains. These pilgrimages were in honour of the ancient pagan god Lugh, who is said to have held a great feast and athletics trials (which included scaling a mountain), after his mother's funeral. Pilgrimages remain significant, albeit Christianised, and today they honour Irish saints (pilgrimpath.ie).

24 Dingle Views & **BAR PEWS**

PANORAMIC VIEWS | PUB LIFE

▬▬▬ Tipped as 'the most beautiful place on earth' by *National Geographic*, the Dingle Peninsula has some of the most breathtaking scenery in Ireland. Even in the rain there's beauty around every corner and there's a pub to suit every mood.

🧭 How to

Getting around The nearest train stations are at Tralee and Killarney; direct buses to Dingle take six hours from Dublin. There is a local bus service on the peninsula (locallink kerry.ie), but having a car guarantees more time and flexibility.

When to go Sunny days are so random in Ireland that you can be lucky any time of year. July and August brings heavy traffic.

What to wear Pack walking boots, rainwear and warm layers as some viewpoints can get very windy and wet.

Walking the wild side Sheltered between the foot of Mt Brandon and the wide arc of Brandon Bay, the **Cloghane and Brandon** area is Dingle Peninsula's wilder side. It's a walker's paradise and there are cosy pubs to rest feet, sink a pint and tuck into a delicious meal. **Murphy's Bar** is right on the pier in Brandon, perfect for an outdoor pint overlooking beautiful Brandon Bay. In Cloghane, **O'Connor's Bar** is one of Ireland's oldest pubs, offering a warm welcome and pints by the fire.

Edge of the world The road ends at **Brandon Point**, with only the wild Atlantic beyond and dolphins in the waves below. Walk up to the old WWII watchtower and stand in awe. On a clear day you can see as far north as County Clare. **Mt Brandon** is a popular mountain climb, best attempted using **Faha Car Park** as the starting point. With the right gear and

✓ Local Tips

Secret Bay Park at Teer Cross and walk for around an hour (4km) along part of the Dingle Way to stand high above secluded Sás Creek.

Ancient Tomb The dramatic valley of Loch a'Dúin contains over 80 stone-age structures, including a mini Newgrange – a tomb illuminated by the setting sun of the autumn equinox.

Recommended by Micheál O'Dowd, owner of O'Connor's Bar & Guesthouse @micheal.odowd

Left O'Connor's Bar **Above left** Brandon Harbour **Above right** Mt Brandon

weather the views are worth the sore limbs, but it's a strenuous trip and can be dangerous in poor conditions – get local advice before setting off. It's approximately 11km out and back with a gradient of over 900m, so allow at least five hours in daylight to complete the hike.

Ireland's longest beach Pink-gold sand stretches 14km from **Fermoyle Beach** out to a sandy strip called the **Maharees**, a playground of pristine Atlantic waves and rolling dunes as far as the eye can see. At the end, you'll happily drown your salty lips with a cold pint at **Spillane's Bar**. At sunset, the view back across the bay to Mount Brandon and Brandon Point is a special experience.

Heady heights Sandwiched between the mountainside and a sheer drop to the valley below, **Connor Pass** is Ireland's highest mountain pass. Take the easy road (around a 10-minute drive) from Dingle to the top for jaw-dropping scenery to the north and south

🥾 Hiking Caherconree

Caherconree mountain pass is the rougher, older brother of Connor Pass – and less of a show-off. This scenic 'road of the stones' winds through the majestic Slieve Mish Mountains from Camp to just east of Inch Beach. Stop at the signpost for **Caherconree Promontory Fort**, strap on your boots and follow the trail up to see the remains of Ireland's highest stone fort (683m), home of the fabled sorcerer and high king of Munster, Cú Roí. It can be a tricky ascent in wet weather as the ground can be too boggy to cross but, when it's clear, the views of Dingle Bay and the Iveragh Peninsula are majestic.

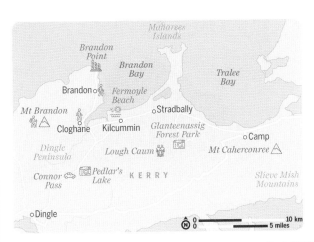

Left Views from Caherconree **Below** Dick Mack's

If you do tackle the narrow road down, stop at the small car park by a waterfall. It's worth the rocky scramble to **Pedlar's Lake** above it for unparalleled views across the valley.

Settle your nerves In Dingle you are spoiled for choice for pubs after a long day's drive. **O'Sullivan's Courthouse** and **Foxy John's** are both excellent for creamy pints of the black stuff and great local banter. For something stronger, century-old **Dick Mack's** has a wall of whiskies, retaining its reputation as the best whiskey bar in Ireland. The live traditional music scene in Dingle's pubs is hard to beat and easily found.

Land before time It feels like the glaciers have just receded when you take in the scenery at **Glanteenassig Forest Park**, where huge dark corrie lakes are framed by steep rocky cliffs. There are excellent walks of all grades and kids love the fairy-tale boardwalk around **Lough Caum**. End the day with a fireside pint at **Ashes Pub** in the village of Camp.

The Emerald Galaxy

WHEN STAR WARS CAME TO KERRY

Between 2014 and 2016, Hollywood descended on the isolated rock of Skellig Michael twice to transform it into the first Jedi temple. Visitors have since flooded the area in search of *Star Wars*, and the local community has adapted to living with its movie fame.

Left and right Skellig Michael
Middle The Moorings

BRIAN KELLY/EYEEM/GETTY IMAGES ©

Why Kerry?

As the sacred home of early Christian monks, there's little surprise that *Star Wars* location scouts were drawn in by the mystical allure of **Skellig Michael** off Kerry's remote Atlantic coast. Seemingly impenetrable, moody and lashed by the Atlantic, the skellig sits alone 12km offshore at Ireland's most southwesterly point. Occupied by monks until around the 12th century, the former monastery and most of the island was declared a Unesco World Heritage Site in 1996.

Because of the day-to-day difficulties of ferrying people to and from the island (often in tempestuous conditions), it was considered a brave decision from Lucasfilm to commit to getting an entire film crew out there. The skellig makes its on-screen debut in *Star Wars: The Force Awakens (Episode VII)* as the first Jedi temple of Ach-To, where Rey (played by Daisy Ridley) eventually tracks down Luke Skywalker (played by Mark Hamill). It then appears again in key scenes of *Star Wars: The Last Jedi (Episode VIII)*.

Community Involvement

During filming, a 2-mile exclusion zone was set up around the island, patrolled by a naval boat. But that didn't mean that locals of the Iveragh Peninsula, off which Skellig Michael sits, were excluded from the action. The crew and cast visited the local school and some were accommodated and fed at the award-winning **The Moorings** in Portmagee. Owners Gerard and Patricia Kennedy also hosted the movie wrap party at the hotel that year, and still regale visitors with the story of Mark Hamill learning to pour a pint of Guinness in their Bridge Bar. Rather than being starstruck, Patricia remembers one local 'totally uninterested', with his back to the famous Jedi as if he was any other barman.

When the *Star Wars* crew returned in 2016 to film *The Last Jedi*, they built a replica of the Skellig Michael monastic site to get around the fact that shooting times were restricted by the weather-dependent ferry crossings to the island. The replica was on **Ceann Sibéal headland** near the village of **Baile an Fheirtéaraigh** (Ballyferriter) and filming took place around a farm run by the Devane family. Local Breege Granville remembers how the rural setting affected some of the film workers from inner-city Dublin, recalling encounters with cows that made 'the boys take off running'.

> The *Star Wars* connection has led to a massive boost in visitors to the area.

The Lucasfilm Effect

According to the Kennedys, the *Star Wars* connection has led to a massive boost in visitors to the area. Their hotel now runs a popular **Star Wars Package** (moorings.ie/star-wars-the-force-awakens), which includes a tour around Skellig Michael (though not a landing) in season.

Pat Devane, owner of the farm used in filming in 2016, has created a **Sunset Site trail** for people to visit the location where Luke Skywalker fades into 'the force', not far from the summit of Ceann Sibéal.

In 2018, local fans helped launch the **May the 4th Festival**, which now runs annually in Ballyferriter, Portmagee, Ballinskelligs and Valentia Island. The festival coincides with Féile na Bealtaine, the Celtic celebrations marking the start of summer. Local communities blend the two festivals with unique cultural crossovers, such as the Kerry School of Music playing the *Star Wars* scores and local Irish dancers performing in *Star Wars* costumes.

⛵ Touring Skellig Michael

It's an unforgettable experience landing on Skellig Michael (possible mid-May to September). There are 600 stone steps to climb, hand-carved by monks in the 6th century, to reach the monastic site with its famous beehive huts 150m above the sea. As visitor numbers are restricted, booking in advance is absolutely essential. Note that trips can be cancelled in bad weather. It's best to stay the night before in or near Portmagee as boats don't wait if you're late. Skelligmichael.com has a list of tour operators and a comprehensive guide to the Skelligs. Eco tours around the islands are a wonderful alternative if landing isn't possible.

WILDLIFE
of Kerry

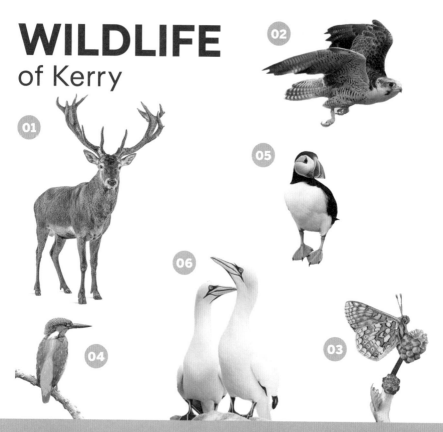

01 Red deers
Killarney National Park is home to the last surviving herd of indigenous red deer in Ireland (herds in other counties were reintroduced using Scottish deer).

02 Peregrine falcons
These raptors are the world's fastest flying bird, with the potential to reach speeds of up to 320km/h while diving for prey.

03 Marsh fritillaries
This beautifully patterned butterfly can be found in the Killarney valley. Look out for them in May and June.

04 Kingfishers
This distinctive bird is found throughout Ireland, and can be spotted by the Deenagh, Cloghereen and Gearhameen rivers in County Kerry.

05 Puffins
Between April and August, puffins breed in colonies on the Skelligs and Blasket Islands.

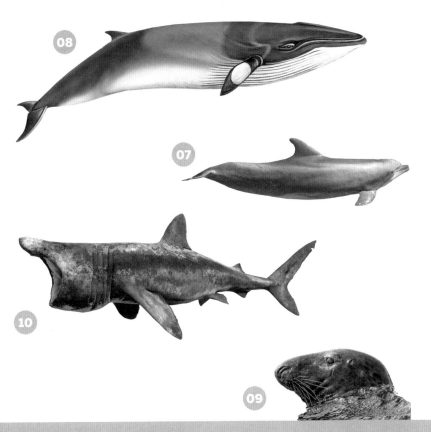

Once the puffling chicks have fledged, the puffins return to sea.

06 Gannets

Ireland's largest colony of nesting gannets is on Little Skellig, where tens of thousands of seabirds gather during the summer breeding season.

07 Dolphins

The common dolphin is frequently seen swimming off the Kerry coast. It's also possible to spot the acrobatic breaches of bottlenose dolphins.

08 Minke whales

This species can be recognised by the white band that wraps around each flipper. They are most often seen between April and July.

09 Grey seals

Great Blasket Island is home to Ireland's largest grey seal breeding colony. In autumn furry pups can be spotted.

10 Basking sharks

The waters around the Kerry coast are often visited by basking sharks, who swim around open-mouthed catching plankton.

The Dolphin that put Dingle on the Map

HOW FUNGIE'S FAME CHANGED A TOWN

It's rare for a dolphin to stay solo for long in one area. Yet, in Dingle, Fungie found his pod of two-legged landlubbers, sea-farers and swimmers and never wanted to leave. He made it into the *Guinness Book of Records* for longest-living solitary dolphin, but disappeared in 2020.

Left Fungie **Middle** Dingle Harbour Lighthouse **Right** Oceanworld Aquarium

For local residents, Fungie has been synonymous with Dingle for decades. Councillor Breandán Fitzgerald, who is from Dingle and was 10 when Fungie arrived almost 40 years ago, says: 'If anyone asked you where you're from, you'd say Dingle, then they'd smile and say "Fungie, the Dingle Dolphin"'.

When Fungie showed up in 1983, it was a time of deep recession and emigration in Ireland. Livelihoods in Dingle centred on fishing and agriculture, both in decline at the time. Breandán believes Fungie was fundamental to the change of fortunes for the community. 'It was retired fishermen who were bringing people out...they were able to make a living and their children were able to make a living,' he says.

Breandán saw, first-hand, the effect Fungie had on people staying at his guesthouse. It became apparent that anyone who encountered Fungie went home with a memory of a lifetime, and spread the news about their experience. 'People would come down on holidays and see the dolphin...they just wouldn't be able to stop talking about the trip,' he recalls.

Fungie's fame secured a future for generations of fam-ilies. Thousands of people every year, over three decades, visited the area to see him, creating an entire tourism industry around the playful dolphin.

Jimmy Flannery established **Dingle Dolphin Tours** (dingledolphin.com) in 1987 and says he believes 'Fungie did more for Dingle than any tourist board could have'.

POTSTOCK/SHUTTERSTOCK ©

KENNETH GINN/GETTY IMAGES ©

Deep Connection

Fungie became part of the fabric of the community of Dingle and the town didn't just gain economically. To many, he became a comforting presence in the harbour, even a lifelong friend. Fishermen leaving the harbour, possibly facing a dangerous journey at sea, were accompanied by Fungie on their way out and welcomed back with excited jumps on their return.

> Thousands of people every year, over three decades, visited the area to see him.

One day, Fungie just disappeared. Jimmy says that although he always knew someday Fungie would be gone, the sense of loss he feels is palpable. 'It hits now and again. I've been taking people out for 33 years and everywhere you look in the house, there's pictures of Fungie, Fungie with my kids... he's everywhere. It's really like losing a member of the family'.

Fungie's disappearance has had an impact on the dolphin boat tour operators, with half of them deciding to drop anchor, but Jimmy has set up **Dingle Sea Safaris** to show visitors the peninsula's impressive abundance of marine life.

Marine biologist Kevin Flannery says marine life is actually on the rise. 'There's a lot more. For the first time ever, the week Fungie disappeared we had minke whales in the mouth of Dingle Harbour,' he says. Kevin was inspired by Fungie to open Dingle's **Oceanworld Aquarium**. Both he and Jimmy believe that the popularity of eco trips and wildlife tours in Dingle, and all around Ireland's coast, wouldn't have happened without Fungie.

🐟 Life after Fungie

Jimmy plans to organise a mural of Fungie on the gable of **Dingle Harbour Lighthouse** and hopefully, in the future, a sea wildlife awareness weekend in Dingle, dedicated to Fungie.

There's still an exciting amount of marine life to encounter, and the boat operators traversing the coast and the Blasket Islands have years of experience thanks to Fungie's presence.

On a **Dingle Sea Safari** (dingleseasafari.com) there's a chance to regularly see common dolphins, a huge seal colony and puffins. Minke, humpback and fin whales show up seasonally and sometimes even orca can be found here. 'That's Fungie's legacy,' says Jimmy.

Listings

BEST OF THE REST

Parks & Family Attractions

Kells Bay Gardens

Perfect for young intrepid explorers. Enjoy strolling through peaceful woodland and spotting large carved dinosaurs, then stroll to the secluded beach a 10-minute walk away.

Bonane Heritage Park

One of Kerry's most significant archaeological sites, where the Ring of Kerry and Ring of Beara meet. There's a spectacular summer solstice alignment here in June.

Killarney National Park

Families can enjoy a horse-drawn tour by jaunting car, roam the extensive grounds to find wild deer and take a tour with Muckross Traditional Farms to learn about 1930s and 1940s rural Ireland.

Glenbeigh Fairy Forest

Take a leisurely stroll through this forest to discover around 50 fairy huts, 1km from Glenbeigh Village. Entertaining for young ones with imagination.

Gleninchaquin Park

Right on the Beara Peninsula, this family-run park has a mix of easy sloping terrains, cascading waterfalls, and serene woodland as well as more challenging walking routes.

Kerry Dishes & Coffee

Jack's Coastguard Restaurant €€

Perfect stop on the Ring of Kerry with panoramic sea and mountain views, serving Irish dishes such as seafood specialities and local Kerry lamb. In a former station dating to 1866.

Parkgate Coffee

Popular takeaway coffee spot with queues out the door. Grab your coffee and take a stroll to nearby Tralee Town Park.

Sol y Sombra €€

Sip cocktails and indulge in tapas (pork belly, scallops, tostadas) at this restaurant built into the atmospheric renovated church in downtown Killorglin. Live gigs throughout the year.

Bean in Dingle

Bright, smart coffee shop with hot brews and sweet treats. Queues are worth the wait on Green St.

The Smugglers Inn €€€

This Waterville restaurant is well known for serving up top-class food presented with style, overlooking the serene beach at Ballinskelligs. Garden for alfresco dining.

Beaufort Bar & Restaurant €€

This bar dates back to 1841 and serves up local Irish food, including a delicious rack of Kerry lamb.

Perfect Pubs, Pints & Tipples

Tigh TP

Sink a pint or two with beautiful views across the water while sitting outside TP's in Baile an nGall (Ballydavid), followed by a walk on the beach.

John B Keane's Pub

Savour slow-poured pints and great conversation in this intimate establishment in Listowel, run by the family of one of Ireland's most celebrated playwrights.

Tigh an tSaorsaigh

Many visitors love this great Irish pub in Baile an Fheirtéaraigh (Ballyferriter). Right in the West Kerry Gaeltacht, expect animated discussions and tasty drinks.

Crowley's Bar

Drinks are always flowing in Kenmare at this lively establishment with traditional music and song. A night out not to be missed.

PF McCarthy's

A long-established, lively pub in Kenmare with live music. Perfect for groups, dates, or a solo night out.

Arts & Pottery

Cill Rialaig Arts Centre

Contemporary, creative space five minutes from Ballinskellig beach, where artists from across the world exhibit their work. On-site cafe, shop and children's workshops.

Louis Mulcahy Pottery

A delightful pottery shop with on-site cafe near Ballyferrriter. Robust stoneware porcelain from dining sets to colourful urns. Ships around the world.

Greenlane Gallery

Distinguished and distinctive artists display their work here (paintings, sculptures, jewellery), including world-renowned Liam O'Neill. Right in the heart of Dingle.

Siamsa Tíre

The National Folk Theatre is in Tralee Town Park. Expect everything from musicals to dramatic pieces, as well as an airy gallery space.

Kerry Culture & History

Gallarus Oratory

This much visited site is one of the best-preserved early Christian churches in Ireland,

John B Keane's Pub

built between the 7th and 8th centuries. It's on the Slea Head Drive (p152).

Staigue Fort

West of Sneem, this impressive ancient monument has a commanding view of the bay. It's well maintained and has a circular rampart surrounded by an external bank.

Skellig Experience

Exhibitions on the history of the monks on the isolated island, wildlife and lighthouses. It's on Valentia Island; worth visiting if you can't get to Skellig Michael.

Crag Cave

This ancient cave system, thought to be over a million years old, was once full of water and houses beautiful stalagmites and stalactites. Less than five minutes from Castleisland.

Kerry County Museum

An interpretative experience in Tralee, with a focus on archaeology and exploration. Its award-winning Tom Crean Exhibition tells the story of the heroic Irish Antarctic explorer.

Scan for things to see, do and try in Kerry

25

Meander the
SHANNON

WATERWAYS | SCENERY | HISTORY

Meandering through 11 counties on its 360km journey to the sea, the majestic River Shannon is Ireland's longest. Recently listed among the world's most scenic river journeys, the 'Wise River' can be your waymarker to discover Ireland's hidden heartlands.

🗺 How to

Getting here/around
Carrick-on-Shannon is Ireland's cruising capital and is linked by direct train and bus services from Dublin. Here you can arrange river cruises and excursions (waterwaysireland.org).

When to go Summer (June to August, peak season and school holidays) has the best weather and longest days. Prepare for all weather conditions whenever you visit and pack insect repellent in summer. Consider May or September to avoid crowds and midges.

Ancient Settlements to Modern Communities

The mighty River Shannon was a vital waterway and trading route for centuries. Nowadays the Shannon and its lakes are popular for fishing, stunning scenery and a variety of activities both on and off the water, including kayaking, SUP, cycling and hiking. Bluewaysireland.org is a good trip-planning resource.

Lough Derg, the largest of the Shannon's three lakes, is home to some 376 islands, the most notable being **Inis Cealtra** (Holy Island). Lesser known than Clonmacnoise further north on the banks of the Shannon, this 6th-century monastic settlement features four high crosses, a holy well, the ruins of a round tower and several small churches. Although it's now uninhabited, except by some intrepid

🍺 A Pint in Ireland's Oldest Pub

An evening in the pub is a quintessential Irish experience. Believed to be in existence for over a thousand years, Sean's Bar in Athlone holds the Guinness World Record for oldest pub in Ireland, and possibly the world. It doesn't get more traditional than that.

Left Athlone **Above left** River Shannon
Above right Sean's Bar, Athlone

grazing cattle and sheep, funerals still take place in the graveyard with mourners transported from the mainland on small boats. Boat trips to the island leave from **Mountshannon Harbour**.

Up until the 20th century, the 'wise river' operated as a transport channel, and today numerous bustling harbour towns and quaint villages still line its banks. Picturesque **Killaloe** on the banks of Lough Derg was the birthplace of Brian Ború, High King of Ireland (r 1002-14).

Brian lived and reigned from the village, briefly making it Ireland's capital. The 12th-century **St Flannan's Cathedral**, which houses a carved Ogham Stone discovered in 1916 and dated to 1000 CE, will delight history buffs. Killaloe is linked with neighbouring town **Ballina** by an impressive 13-arch stone bridge, which also links the counties of Clare and Tipperary. Join locals jumping off the bridge to cool off on a (rare) warm summer's day.

☰ Experience Lough Ree

The other Nessie Lesser known than its Scottish counterpart, the Lough Ree monster's earliest mention dates back to the 7th century. More recently in 1960, three priests were fishing and one spotted a large black creature 6ft in length swimming up the lough. Head to Athlone to spot Ireland's answer to Nessie.

Birdwatching Keen birders will twitch at Lough Ree, designated a Special Protection Area for its population of migratory waterfowl. The migratory season starts in March.

Family fun For a unique family day out, check out Baysports (baysports.ie) on the lake – Ireland's largest inflatable water park.

Modern Marvels, Mother Nature

Nearing the Atlantic, seabirds and wildlife populate the Shannon estuary's mudflats and manufactured marvels appear.

Harnessing H2O Regarded as a major engineering feat of the 20th century, the **Ardnacrusha Power Station** (esb.ie) was the largest, most powerful hydroelectric power plant in the world when completed in 1929. Today, it's still operational and visitors can sign up for a tour.

Getting airborne The village of Foynes has a unique claim to fame. The first commercial passenger flight between New York and Europe landed here in 1939 using the Shannon as a watery runway. **Foynes Flying Boat & Maritime Museum** is one of a kind and houses the world's only full-size replica of a Boeing B314 – a must for aviation enthusiasts. These transatlantic seaplanes were the absolute height of luxury in their day.

For a modern luxury experience, stay in nearby Adare Manor, an architecturally astounding 19th-century home, restored to five-star hotel standards.

Wild Atlantic The Shannon culminates at Loop Head (loophead.ie). The rugged coastal beauty here is breathtaking and much lesser known than the nearby Cliffs of Moher. Don't miss the Kilkee Cliffs and Bridges of Ross for jaw-dropping views. Keep your eyes peeled for dolphins.

If driving, save time and take the Shannon Ferry between Tarbert and Killimer (shannonferries.com).

Left Lough Ree **Right** Ogham stone, St Flannan's Cathedral

WEST OF IRELAND

NATURE | CLIFFS | MUSIC

Connemara National Park

WEST OF IRELAND
Trip Builder

▬▬▬▬ The West of Ireland is full of adventure. Follow the trail of a pirate queen in County Mayo, take to the waves for surfing, or visit County Clare to cruise under giant sea cliffs and admire wild flowers in the Burren's limestone fissures.

Mullet Peninsula

Ballycroy National Park

Achill Island

Atlantic Ocean

Visit pirate queen Grace O'Malley's castle on **Clare Island** (p196)
🕐 ½ day

Clare Island

Inishturk

Inishbofin

Killary Harbour

Learn how traditional drums are made at a bodhrán workshop in **Roundstone** (p187)
🕐 ½ day

Maumturk Mountains

● Roundstone

Stop for a swim in the clear waters of **Fanore Beach** (p193)
🕐 ½ day

Gorumna Island

Aran Islands

Walk the **Cliffs of Moher** and then cruise under them (p188)
🕐 1 day

Watch big-wave surfers or try freediving at **Mullaghmore** (p198)
🕐 ½ day

Spot seabirds and marine life on a sea kayaking trip from **Rosses Point** (p199)
🕐 ½ day

Take a surfing lesson in **Strandhill** and then have a seaweed bath (p198)
🕐 ½ day

Hear traditional live music sessions in the pubs of **Galway** (p186)
🕐 2 hr

Take up the challenge of the 26km **Black Head Loop** hike (p192)
🕐 1 day

Admire the wild flowers while wandering in **The Burren** (p192)
🕐 ½ day

Mullaghmore
Cliffony
Lower Lough Erne
NORTHERN IRELAND
Lough Melvin
Dartry Mountains
Rosses Point
Sligo Bay
Sligo
Strandhill
Killala Bay
LEITRIM
Lough Allen
Ballina
SLIGO
Lough Conn
Mt Nephin
Nephin Beg Range
ROSCOMMON
MAYO
Castlebar
Westport
Longford
LONGFORD
Lough Ree
Partry Mountains
Lough Mask
WESTMEATH
Lough Corrib
Athlone
GALWAY
Galway
Galway Bay
Kilcolgan
Black Head
Ballyvaughan
Lisdoonvarna
The Burren
Lough Derg
Cliffs of Moher
CLARE

MARK_GUSEV/SHUTTERSTOCK ©,
TERRY HARRIS/ALAMY STOCK PHOTO ©,
HUGH BRYCE/500PX/GETTY IMAGES ©,
MIKROMAN6/GETTY IMAGES ©

0 — 40 km
0 — 20 miles

Practicalities

ARRIVING

By air There are international airports at Shannon in County Clare and Knock in County Mayo.

By train Sligo, Westport, Galway and Limerick are the main train stations.

By car The main motorways are the M4/M6 from Dublin to Galway, the M7 to Limerick and the M18 linking Galway and Limerick.

HOW MUCH FOR A

Half-dozen oysters €13

Bowl of chowder €8

Surfboard rental €20

GETTING AROUND

Car The best option for sightseeing and flexibility to stop at scenic viewpoints.

Bus There are bus connections between main towns. Check buseireann.ie or private operators for routes and timetables.

Bicycle A popular way to get around, with several on- and off-road signed routes to explore.

WHEN TO GO

JAN - MAR

The coldest months; evenings noticeably brighter after March.

APR - JUN

Longer, warmer days towards June, but risk of showers.

JUL - SEP

Warmest, with long summer nights. Always expect rain.

OCT - DEC

Stronger wind and waves. Much cooler, especially in December.

EATING & DRINKING

Galway oysters The city is famed for oysters, with an annual festival celebrating them every September.

Smoked fish Buy direct from smokehouses in the Burren and Connemara, or from local delis.

Achill Island Sea Salt A natural product, harvested in small batches from the Atlantic waters off Achill Island.

Calvey's mountain lamb Sweetened by heather and salty air.

Must-try seafood chowder
Doolin (p202)

Best for honey
The Burren (p202)

CONNECT & FIND YOUR WAY

Wi-fi Available at most accommodations, but unlikely to be high speed. It can be difficult to pick up a phone signal in very remote areas, and 3G/4G coverage can be patchy or non-existent in parts of Connemara and the Burren.
Navigation If you are hiking or exploring remote areas and using your phone to navigate, have backup maps and communication.

GREAT WESTERN GREENWAY

This 44km off-road cycling trail follows the route of the former Westport–Achill Railway. Bike rental is available in Westport (greenway.ie).

WHERE TO STAY

Cities and towns can get busy around festival times and in July, August and bank holidays, so book well in advance.

Place	Pro/Con
Galway City	A good base for food and nightlife. Plenty of accommodation options in the city, from hostels to five-star hotels. Can get busy during festivals and events.
Connemara	Good for rural stays. Look for quiet country houses, glamping and B&Bs.
Westport Town	A lively spot; good base for exploring the area, with plenty of accommodation, pub and restaurant options.
Sligo	Good midrange choices in the town, or around the county. Remote B&Bs, country houses and quirky glampsites.

MONEY

Credit and debit cards are widely accepted and you will find ATMs in the main towns.

26 Galway Pubs & REELS

MUSIC | CULTURE | NIGHTLIFE

Wandering around the pubs of Galway to hear traditional Irish music is a fun experience, as there are live sessions of jigs and reels every night. Hearing instruments like the fiddle (violin), accordion, bodhrán and banjo in full flow will get your feet tapping – these are often accompanied by the tin whistle, flute and uillean pipes (Irish bagpipes).

LES GIBBON/ALAMY STOCK PHOTO ©

🗺 How to

Getting around Most live music venues are in the city centre, which is easy to navigate on foot.

When to go Galway can be busy in high season, on bank holiday weekends and during festivals and the Galway Races.

How much? Most live traditional music sessions in pubs are free; the cost of other music gigs varies per venue.

GERARD PLAUCHE/GETTY IMAGES ©

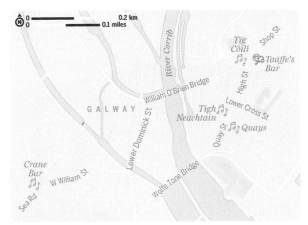

Far left top The Quays Far left bottom Uillean pipes

'Music is a big part of the culture of Galway. There's a lot of soul,' says Galwayman Johnny 'Ringo' McDonagh, a world-famous bodhrán player who has toured the world with Dé Danann and *Riverdance*. Here, he shares his favourite Galway pubs.

Atmosphere One of Johnny's favourites to play traditional music in is **Tig Chóilí** (Mainguard St), which has two trad sessions a day. 'It has a great atmosphere. Lots of well-known musicians join in,' he says. 'Sometimes it gets so crowded with musicians, there might be 10 musicians waiting to play.' Johnny's tip is to visit on a quiet day like a Monday.

Relaxing Sundays Try the **The Crane Bar** (Sea Rd), which has sessions every night, an afternoon session at weekends and a famous Sunday morning session. 'It's very welcoming and homely, there's a great vibe in the place on a Sunday morning, it's very relaxed,' says Johnny.

Singing Popular with GAA sports fans and busy on weekends, **Taaffes Bar** (Shop St) is recommended by Johnny for nightly trad sessions and ballad bands. 'You find a lot of different types of musicians at the trad session,' says Johnny.

History Don't miss **Tigh Neachtain** (Cross St), which dates to 1894 and is at the heart of the Galway music scene, with many famous musicians dropping in. Even older is **The Quays** (Quay St), which dates back 400 years and has Irish and international bands playing every night of the week.

🎵 Beating the Bodhrán

This traditional Irish drum is beaten on one side with a 'tipper'. It is made from goatskin that is specially treated and then stretched over a wood frame. A good place to learn about it is at the Connemara workshop of Ireland's master bodhrán maker, Malachy Kearns, who has been crafting instruments for more than 40 years. His bodhráns have gone on to star in everything from *Riverdance* to the movie *Titanic*. The workshop in Roundstone, County Galway (bodhran. com), is open seven days with a viewing area to look at bodhrán making. Book in advance for a talk on bodhráns and their history.

Cruising the
CLIFFS

WALKING | CLIFFS | NATURE

Experience the thrill of walking along the Cliffs of Moher – magnificent sea cliffs that stretch for 8km along the County Clare coast and plunge 214m into the powerful Atlantic Ocean – or soak up their mightiness from sea-level on a cliff cruise.

🗺️ How to

Getting around Start the walk from the Hag's Head car park. To return, there's a shuttle bus between Doolin, the visitor centre and Hag's Head from June to August.

When to go March to October. As Ireland's most visited natural attraction, it's busy at weekends and in summer. Arrive early morning or late afternoon to avoid crowds.

Boat trips Leave from Doolin; the walk here from Hag's Head is around 14km.

Cliffs of Moher walk Start at **Hag's Head**, the most southerly point of the cliffs. It takes around two hours to walk the 6km from here to the main visitor centre. You'll see **Moher Tower**, the ruin of an old watchtower.

While you walk, you can admire the three Aran Islands in Galway Bay and, on a clear day, see right across Galway Bay to the Twelve Pins and Maumturks mountain range in Connemara National Park. To the south, you might see as far as Loop Head and beyond to County Kerry.

Wildlife The area is teeming with wildlife. You'll see and hear some of the thousands of seabirds – ledges on the cliffs provide nesting sites for more than 20 species, which are in residence from around April to the beginning of August. June or July are the best months to see them and you will need binoculars.

📷 Best Light for Photography

If you're photographing the cliffs, afternoon or evening is the best time, when they are lit up by the evening sun. Always take care, as cliff edges can be unstable. 'If you're taking photos of the cliffs in the morning, you need overcast weather, not blue sky,' says local walking guide Cormac McGinley.

Left Boat trip to the Cliffs of Moher **Above left** Cliffs of Moher **Above right** O'Brien's Tower (p190)

'There are three or four wild goats living on the cliff face, keep an eye out for them,' says Cormac McGinley from **Cormac's Coast** (cormacscoast.com) walking tours. Wild flowers, such as sea pink, birdsfoot trefoil, sea campion and some orchids, also cling to the cliffs.

Geology Local Liscannor stone has been used for walls along the walk. 'Keep an eye out for trace fossils in the stone,' says Cormac. 'They are animal tracks – squiggly lines seen in the cliffs – from animals that died 300 million years ago.'

The **Cliffs of Moher Visitor Centre** (cliff sofmoher.ie) displays more information about the geology of the cliffs. **O'Brien's Tower** nearby was built as a viewing tower in 1835, with the best views from the top.

Cruise the Cliffs

Take a cruise along the Cliffs of Moher with **Doolin2Aran Ferries** (doolin2aranferries

🖊 Birds at the Cliffs of Moher

Atlantic puffins winter at sea and return to nest on grassy cliff ledges. Most visible in June and July.

Peregrine falcons are here year-round. They can reach speeds of up to 240km/h – the fastest animal on the planet.

Red-billed chough, also known as the Celtic Crow, is an endangered species that can be found at the cliffs year-round.

Guillemots live at sea and only come to land to nest, laying their eggs on the cliffs. There are tens of thousands of them, most visible in May and June.

Recommended by marine biologist Cormac McGinley of Cormac's Coast @cormacscoast

com) or **Doolin Ferry Co** (doolinferry.com) to get close to the massive rock faces and to really appreciate the height of these huge grey rock walls from the sea. The boat trips start and end in the village of Doolin and will take you along the cliffs as far as Hag's Head.

Stacks and arches Travelling by boat, you'll see how the power of the Atlantic waves has created magnificent rock formations, like the sea stack **An Branán Mór** and sea arches such as the one under Moher Tower. Rocky ledges provide shelter and nesting sites for up to 30,000 breeding pairs of seabirds.

Cruises pass the highest point of the cliffs at **Knockardakin**, near O'Brien's Tower, which rise 214m above sea level. Look out for sea caves along the way, including the cave that featured as the Horcrux cave in the film *Harry Potter and the Half-Blood Prince*. Occasionally seals, dolphins or basking sharks are spotted from the cruises too.

Trips take around one hour. They are seasonal from March to October and are weather-dependant. Both ferries also run trips from Doolin to the nearby Aran Islands.

Left Peregrine falcon **Right** An Branán Mór

28 Walk the Rocky **BURREN**

OUTDOORS | NATURE | DAY TRIP

████████ Nothing will prepare you for the stark, grey limestone plateaus of the Burren in County Clare, which translates from Irish as 'rocky place'. Hike here to experience the limestone pavements and delicate flora and fauna, while soaking up coastal views.

MNSTUDIO/SHUTTERSTOCK ©

🗺 **How to**

Getting around Start and finish the walk to Black Head at Fanore Beach car park. Most of the walk is off-road and should take around one hour each way.

When to go Between spring and autumn; the best time to see the wild flowers in bloom is around May.

Top tips Keep a look out for wild goats. Leave no trace of your visit and don't move any rocks or stones on the limestone pavement.

🚶 **Hike the Black Head Loop**

This challenging 26km trail goes around **Black Head** and through the **Gleninagh Pass** and **Feenagh Valley**. Terrain varies from grassy tracks to mountain paths and can be rough and overgrown in places. Set aside six to eight hours, take a trail map and wear hiking boots.

GALWAY

04 Stop at the tip of **Black Head** to soak up the views of Black Head Lighthouse and out over Galway Bay to the three Aran Islands.

Galway Bay

02 Look down into the grykes (crevices) between the limestone clints (slabs) to spot **rare wild flowers** – orchids, gentians, mountain avens and bloody cranesbill – brought by birds from Alpine, Arctic and Mediterranean origins.

05 Detour down a grassy lane to **Gleninagh Castle**, a tower house that dates to the late 1500s and overlooks a stony beach. The holy well nearby is said to cure eye ailments.

Black Head

Dobhach Bhráinín

Gleninagh Pass

Blackhead Bay

Feenagh Valley

Gleniunagh Mountain

Cappanawalla

○ Ballyvaughan

Fanore

Ballyreen

The Burren

CLARE

03 Explore the huge flat layers of exposed limestone pavement that reach right down to the shore at **Murrooghtoohy**, with erratics (huge boulders) left behind by the ice age.

South Sound

01 Stroll the golden sands of **Fanore Beach**, swim (or surf) in the clear waters, explore the sand dunes or look for fossils in the limestone bedrock around the beach.

Doolin Point

N
0 — 0
5 miles — 10 km

WILDLIFE
of the Burren

01 Rare flowers

Spring and summer are the best time to see wild flowers like the mountain aven, spring gentian, Irish orchid and bloody cranesbill all in bloom.

02 Irish hares

The coat of the Irish mountain hare is reddish-brown in summer. It's larger than a rabbit and can run up to 60km/h.

03 Butterflies

There are around 30 species of butterfly – look out for the brimstone, which is yellow, or the pearl-bordered fritillary, which is only found here.

04 Red foxes

Red foxes live in dens and are mostly nocturnal, but are sometimes spotted during the day here.

05 Feral goats

There's a herd of feral goats roaming these hills. They're identifiable by their woolly coats and large horns.

06 Bats

There are seven different species of bat in the Burren, including the endangered lesser horseshoe bat, and they hibernate in the area's caves.

07 Birds

There are 100 species, including visiting peregrine falcons and migrating whooper swans. Listen out for the call of the meadow pipit, skylark and cuckoo.

08 Pine martens

These elusive creatures are tricky to spot as they hunt at night. They're the same size as a domestic cat, with a bushy tail.

Grace O'Malley: The Pirate Queen

THE WOMAN WHO RULED BY LAND AND BY SEA

Grace O'Malley, also known as Granuaile, was a powerful female leader who commanded her own army and fleet of galleys. Follow in her footsteps by visiting her castles around the County Mayo coast, and hear stories of how she came to rule in the 16th century.

Left Clare Island **Middle** Wall painting, Cistercian Abbey **Right** Kildavnet Castle

Grace O'Malley, Ireland's 'pirate queen', was born in 1530 into the seafaring Uí Mháille, (O'Malley), clan, who ruled Clew Bay and the surrounding territory, including Clare Island. For generations, they earned their wealth through fishing and trading to Spain and Scotland as well as some plundering and piracy on the side.

Well educated in her youth, Grace, who is also known by the names Gráinne Ní Mháille or Granuaile, chose a career in seafaring, then a bold and dangerous occupation that was considered taboo for a woman. Her ability as an intrepid seafarer and her success as a businesswoman meant that her crew and army of 200 men acknowledged her as their commander and remained loyal to her throughout her long life. With her own ships and crews, she traded and pirated successfully for over 50 years along the coasts of Ireland and Scotland.

On land, Grace became involved in the politics of the period, initially leading her army by land and sea in rebellion against the English invasion of her territory. Later, she used her political acumen to sail to London in 1593 and negotiate directly with Queen Elizabeth I.

Grace married twice and when her second husband, the powerful chieftain Richard-in-Iron Bourke, died in 1583, Grace seized his Rockfleet castle on the north shore of Clew Bay. From here she continued her seafaring activities well into her old age, until her death in 1603. She is buried in the abbey on Clare Island.

As Anne Chambers, author of Grace's biography, discovered in her search for the woman behind the legend, 'Grace O'Malley challenged and triumphed over the boundaries placed in her path, both by man and by nature,

to become the world's first recorded feminist trailblazer. Commanding by sea makes her unique among other female leaders in history. Today, with focus on such issues as gender equality and female empowerment, as well as ageism, this makes her shine as an inspirational beacon to women everywhere.'

> With her own ships and crews, she traded and pirated successfully for over 50 years along the coasts of Ireland and Scotland.

In Grace's Footsteps

You can follow in Granuaile's footsteps on Clare Island, where **Granuaile's Castle**, a 16th-century tower house, overlooks the harbour where Grace's ships once anchored. The nearby **Cistercian Abbey** houses medieval wall paintings, the O'Malley coat of arms with their motto 'Terra Marique Potens' meaning powerful by land and sea, and the tomb said to be Grace O'Malley's final resting place.

On Achill Island, another 15th-century O'Malley tower house, **Kildavnet Castle**, overlooks Achill Sound. **Rockfleet Castle**, Grace O'Malley's last known address, still stands in a quiet inlet of Clew Bay. 'The coastal area associated with Grace O'Malley is undoubtedly one of the most beautiful in Ireland,' says Anne. 'With Clare Island guarding its entrance leading to the historic port of Westport... it's an appropriate setting for a pirate queen.'

⊘ Find Out More

Grace O'Malley: The Biography of Ireland's Pirate Queen 1530–1603 (1979) Author Anne Chambers (graceomalley.com) tells the remarkable true story of this extraordinary leader.

Granuaile Visitor Centre In Louisburgh. A video and exhibition about Grace's life and exploits, as well as about Ireland of the 1500s, the O'Malley Clan, Clew Bay and the surrounding area.

Granuaile Loop Walk Take this 6.7km trail around Achill Island for amazing views of Clew Bay and Achill Sound. The trail starts and ends at Pattens Bar and takes around 2½hours (achilltourism.com).

Westport House The ancestral home of Grace O'Malley's descendants (westporthouse.ie).

29 Surf Sessions
IN SLIGO

SURFING | ADVENTURE | WILD ATLANTIC WAY

▬▬▬ Punctuating the Sligo coastline are countless beach breaks, headlands and reefs that produce some of the best and most consistent surf in the country. From riding the gentle beginner breaks at Enniscrone to watching the world's elite big-wave surfers getting towed into giant barrels at Mullaghmore, Sligo has it all. Start planning your surfari with these epic Irish waves.

GARY MCCALL/SHUTTERSTOCK ©

🗺 **How to**

When to go September to May is the prime time for waves in Ireland, when the Atlantic swells are most powerful, but you can surf year-round.

What to wear You will need at least 3mm of neoprene in summer and autumn, and 5mm in winter and spring. A hood, gloves and booties are advised in the colder months.

Rentals Wetsuits and foam and hard boards can be rented from 7th Wave Surf School in Enniscrone.

MARK DUSE/SHUTTERSTOCK ©

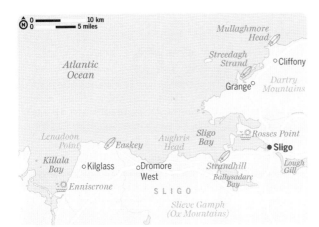

Find Your Perfect Spot

Beginner-friendly breaks Enniscrone and Strandhill are excellent beaches for learners to hone their skills. There are plenty of surf schools at each beach, offering lessons to get you up and riding in the Sligo surf. Due to county regulations, you cannot rent surfboards in Strandhill so if you don't have your own gear, you will need to enrol in a lesson.

Intermediate and advanced The faster waves at Easkey combine barrelling sections with whackable walls that track over the rocky reef. Easkey left, near the river mouth, works best with a high incoming tide while Easkey right, just east of the castle, is a reliable break that can produce picture-perfect tubes in the right conditions. Streedagh Strand also delivers consistent surf with both beach and reef breaks. Northwest-facing Strandhill can hold swells of up to 4ft before maxing out.

One to watch Mullaghmore Head is home to one of the biggest, coldest and heaviest waves on the planet. Waves standing more than 60ft tall are tackled by a handful of the most elite big-wave surfers from Ireland and around the world. Seeing these dedicated athletes brave these huge swells, paddling and towing into gigantic walls of water, is a sight to behold. The surf can be viewed safely from Mullaghmore Head, but be careful as the weather can be wild.

Alternative Sligo Water Adventures

Sea kayaking Get up close and personal with marine and birdlife and witness jaw-dropping scenery by sea kayak. West Coast Kayaking has everything you need to get your paddle adventure started. (westcoast kayaking.ie)

Freediving In Mullaghmore, Freedive Ireland is the country's first freediving school. It provides a range of courses, from one-day experiences to multiday training programs, so you can explore the underwater world on a single breath. (freedive ireland.com)

Kitesurfing Rosses Point is an untouched stretch of beach, perfectly positioned for kitesurfers to enjoy Sligo's prevailing westerlies. You will need your own equipment, as rentals are not available locally.

Listings

BEST OF THE REST

Nature Immersion

Wild Nephin Ballycroy National Park

Start at the visitor centre and then explore more than 150 sq km of Atlantic bogland, mountains and wilderness. Visit the park on a clear night to experience Mayo Dark Sky Park.

Derrigimlagh Bog

Cycle or walk through this section of Galway peat blanket bog, and see the site of the world's first transatlantic radio station and where Alcock and Brown crash landed in 1919 after the first non-stop transatlantic flight.

Westport Cruises

Take a leisurely 1½-hour trip around the hundreds of tiny islands in Clew Bay, meet a local colony of seals and see holy Croagh Patrick mountain from the water.

Connemara National Park

There's lots to see here in Galway's national park, with 2000 hectares of mountains, bog and forest and plenty of rare plant species, birds, rabbits and foxes. If you're lucky, you might even find some Connemara ponies.

Doolin Cave

Go underground and see some of the cave formations beneath the Burren in County Clare – including the Great Stalactite, which hangs down 7.3m, making it Europe's longest free-hanging stalactite.

Killary Harbour

Take to the calm waters of Ireland's longest fjord in a kayak, or soak up the surrounds on a leisurely 90-minute cruise of this 16km-long waterway in County Mayo.

Hazelwood Forest

This gorgeous forest in Sligo is set on the shores of Lough Gill with a lovely view of some of the lake's islands. It's perfect for a peaceful nature walk, with some sculpture along the way.

Inishbofin Island

Take the 30-minute ferry out to the island from Cleggan, 10km northwest of Clifden, and rent a bike or walk the island for nature, unspoilt beaches and the ruins of a castle, an old chapel and a graveyard.

History & Tradition

National Museum of Ireland – Country Life

Wander the folklife collection at this Mayo museum to get a picture of life in rural Ireland in times gone by. You can also explore the mansion house.

Connemara Heritage Centre

Just outside Clifden, this family-run farm and heritage centre is a good spot to learn about the history and traditions of Connemara, with Connemara ponies, donkeys and chickens.

Moyne Friary

Céide Fields

This fascinating heritage site in County Mayo is a record of farming, with the evidence of fields, dwelling areas and tombs dating back 6,000 years to the Stone Age.

The Burren Centre

Visit this centre in Kilfenora, County Clare, for exhibitions and audiovisual recordings to teach you about this unusual rocky landscape, plus a craft shop and tea room.

Connemara Wild Escapes

Step aboard a traditional Galway Hooker sailing boat for a two- or three-hour trip along the Connemara coast to learn all about the maritime traditions of the area.

Killary Sheep Farm

See a demonstration of how the sheepdogs are trained, watch a sheep-shearing demo, see bog cutting in action or go on a countryside walk around Leenane in County Mayo.

Beth Moran Handweaver

If you're taken with the spinning or weaving you see at this studio and shop on Clare Island, you can come back for a weekend or week-long course and learn the craft for yourself.

Moyne Friary

See the impressive ruins of a friary, with well-preserved cloisters, a tower and a church. It dates to 1455 and is one of the largest Franciscan friaries in Ireland.

 Adventure

Croagh Patrick

Climb this holy mountain in Mayo for the views over Clew Bay and its islands from the summit – the terrain is rocky, so bring good hiking shoes and rent a hiking stick at the base.

Delphi Adventure Centre

There's lots to do on both land and water at this Connemara adventure centre, with

Croagh Patrick

kayaking, surfing, climbing and more, plus a spa to unwind in afterwards and overnight accommodation at Delphi Resort.

Northwest Adventure Tours

Go paddleboarding at dawn on Lough Gill, biking in the Sligo hills or on a forest night hike with this adventure company – you can even bike to a paddling session or a seaweed bath.

Great Western Greenway

Walk or cycle this off-road trail from Westport to Achill Island, which runs 42km along an old railway line. It's divided into three stages, with views of the mountains and sea.

Killary Adventure Company

Try a turf challenge obstacle course, gorge walking or a sunset fishing trip – there's even a giant paddleboard to fit all the family in this fun adventure centre just outside Leenane.

Island View Riding Stables

Go horse riding on a County Sligo beach or even to a private island for a picnic – there are rides and treks to suit all levels from beginner to expert.

Pure Magic

Learn to kitesurf, surf or paddleboard on Achill Island in Mayo and then stay overnight at the lodge at the foot of Slievemore mountain, overlooking Keel Lake.

Tour the Land

Scattery Island Tour

Take the short boat trip from Kilrush, County Clare, to this uninhabited island for a walking tour. You'll learn about the island's history and then have some free time to explore and enjoy a picnic.

Mungo Murphy's Seaweed Co

Go on a coastal walk, a wild foraging session and a tasting tour around Connemara to learn about the landscape and its edible sea plants, and to sample local seafood.

Lissadell House

Take a guided tour of this stately home in Sligo, which was the childhood home of revolutionary and politician Constance Markievicz and her sister, suffragist Eva Gore-Booth. Afterwards, stroll the lovely coastal gardens.

Lough Gill Brewery

Learn all about the history of brewing in County Sligo and how the different flavours of craft beer are brewed here – with a few tasting samples along the way.

Electric Escapes

Take your pick of self-guided e-bike tours around the County Mayo landscape and coast – this company will provide you with everything from maps and binoculars to picnics.

Flavours of the West

Galway Food Tours

Try everything from local oysters and beers to local cheeses on this city walk with some tasty stops. The company also runs whiskey tours and cycling food tours.

Westport Food and Craft Market

This market sets up every Saturday (from March) along the riverside on South Mall, with local baking and organic vegetables, plus handmade crafts.

Burren Honey

Gorgeous golden organic honey made from the local wild flowers in the Burren region – depending on the season, the honey can have hints of everything from heather and clover to dandelion and ivy.

Galway Bay Seafoods

Take a two-hour seafood cooking class in Galway's docks – choose from a seafood chowder, lobster, salmon or shellfish workshop – and then tuck into your creations afterwards.

Krēm Gelateria

Local flavours take on sweet form with this homemade gelato using local milk and cream – try the brown bread ice cream or Achill Island Sea Salt caramel flavour. There's coffee and crepes, too.

Clifden Farmers Market

There's everything from the landscape of Connemara here: organic vegetables, herbs, breads, pies and even some clothing. Every Friday morning (June to September).

Aniar Galway

Treat yourself to a Michelin-star meal in Galway using seasonal, wild and foraged food from the local landscape and sea in the West of Ireland. There's also a cookery school here.

Fresh Galway oysters

Hazel Mountain Chocolate

A boutique 'bean to bar' chocolate factory in the Burren, which does everything on-site from roasting the beans to ageing the chocolate. Take a tour, then stock up in the shop.

Connemara Smokehouse

Visit this gorgeous smokehouse on a small pier in Connemara and take a tour to find out how they smoke their delicious salmon, mackerel, tuna and more. You can even meet the original kiln 'Old Smoky'.

Matt Molloy's

Tasty Tipples

Hargadon Bros

This gorgeous old pub in Sligo, a former spirit merchant and grocer dating to 1868, is now a gastropub with lots of wood, snugs and old drawers behind the bar counter.

White Hag Brewery

Look out for this Sligo brewery's local IPAs and lagers in pubs and retail outlets. Its beers are inspired by everything from the Atlantic to local wild berries and sour beers are a speciality.

Micil Distillery

Take a tour and tasting here to find out all about whiskey, *poitín* (an illicit Irish whiskey) and gin. The family story goes back to 1848 and to an ancestor of the head distiller, Pádraic Ó Griallais.

O'Loclainn's Irish Whiskey Bar

Whiskey lovers will be spoilt for choice in this tiny pub in Ballyvaughan, County Clare. Visitors will find shelves full of whiskeys from all over the world, including many old and rare bottles, plus lots of atmosphere.

Matt Molloy's

A lively bar in Westport town, owned by a member of traditional Irish music band the Chieftains. There are live music sessions every night of the week – it gets busy, so arrive early.

Creative Crafts

Foxford Woollen Mills

Foxford in County Mayo is the place for everything wool. Browse for soft lambswool and cashmere throws, and cosy merino wool scarves in a range of colours.

Spiddal Craft Village

Local artists and craft makers populate this village just outside Galway. Take a stroll to find glass, handmade baskets, ceramics, jewellery and clothing with Irish-language expressions.

The Burren Perfumery

Lotions and potions of all types, all created with florals from the local landscape. The small batches of cosmetics and perfumes on offer are made on-site.

Inis Meáin Knitting Co

The contemporary knitwear collections at this studio on Inis Meáin island have been inspired by the landscape, but also by the traditional stitches and clothing styles of the islanders in past times.

30 Festival FEVER

CULTURE | ENTERTAINMENT | ARTS

Culturally and artistically, Ireland has always over-achieved and this is reflected in a huge range of festivals. And, as all locals will tell you, Paddys really know how to party. Time your trip with one of the many festivals on offer and you're guaranteed a good time.

🗺 How to

When to go Most festivals in Ireland run between May and September.

When to book Bigger festivals (such as Electric Picnic, Kilkenny Cat Laughs) usually sell out fast; tickets generally go on sale the winter before.

Top tips For camping festivals, plan to arrive when the campsite opens and avoid locations near the bathrooms. Always pack a raincoat as Irish weather is notoriously changeable.

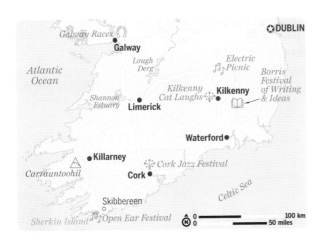

Far left top Electric Picnic **Far left bottom** Fleadh Cheoil na hÉireann

Electric Picnic Ireland's largest arts and music festival is a three-day camping affair, featuring international acts from across the musical divides, local favourites, up-and-coming acts, debate and discussion, cinema and tarot card readers. You can even get married here.

Galway Races Horse racing is synonymous with Ireland and the week-long Galway Races is Ireland's longest racing festival. Food, music and fashion all complement the racing to create an electric atmosphere that draws people from all over the world.

Kilkenny Cat Laughs One of Europe's best-loved comedy festivals. Running since 1995, it's hosted by beautiful medieval Kilkenny and features international and domestic artists, from Eddie Izzard to Tommy Tiernan.

Cork Jazz Festival One of Ireland's flagship arts and cultural events attracting global performers and visitors to more than 90 venues. Much like the musical form of jazz itself, the festival remains fluid, fresh and contemporary.

Fleadh Cheoil na hÉireann The Festival of Music in Ireland is a week-long street fest of traditional Irish music that has been running for over 60 years. The host town changes each year; attendees can wander the in-town locations and listen to the world's best traditional Irish musicians.

Open Ear Festival Presenting the best of Irish experimental music, from avant-garde to electronica. Open Ear is held on Sherkin Island, in Roaringwater Bay off the coast of Cork, making it one of Ireland's most picturesque festivals.

📖 Hedonism & Literary Homage

Leading international creatives descend on the rural hinterland of the Blackstairs Mountains at the invite of **Borris Festival of Writing & Ideas**. It's a literary festival with camping, a dozen food purveyors and a wine sommelier in a 1950s caravan, typically held every June. Previous speakers have included Margaret Atwood, Martin Amis, David Gilmour and Cillian Murphy. As night falls, however, things get a little more hedonistic. As co-founder Hugo Jellett puts it: 'A little bit of Ireland seeps into the bones of the visitors and they forget about everything except right now.'

ULSTER

COASTAL | HISTORY | CULTURE

Carrick-A-Rede rope bridge

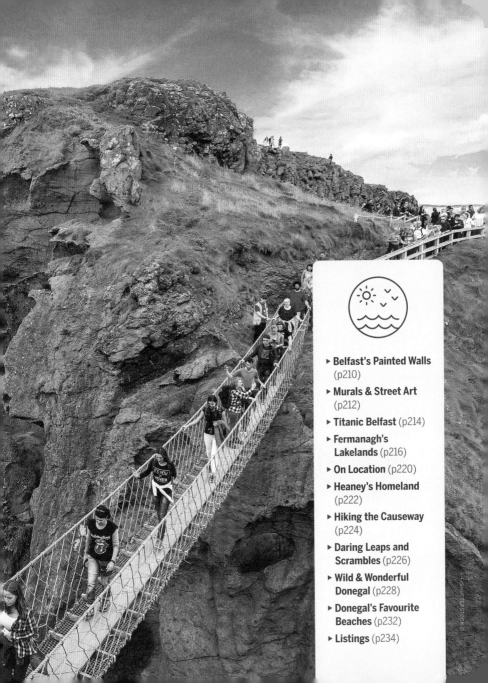

ULSTER
Trip Builder

Explore bookable experiences in Ulster online

0   40 km
0   20 miles

Ulster's spectacular coastline calls out to be explored. Inland, peaceful loughs offer further opportunities for water sports and wildlife spotting. The province's troubled history is reflected in political murals, but a brighter future shines through in its rich cultural life.

Leap into the sea on a Causeway Coast **coasteering** session (p226)
🕐 ½ day

Hike over hexagonal rocks on the **Causeway Coast** (p224)
🕐 1-2 days

Explore the soaring cliffs and pristine beaches of **Donegal** (p228)
🕐 2 days

Visit the places that inspired Seamus Heaney's poetry, near **Bellaghy** (p222)
🕐 1 day

Paddle out to Lough Erne's mysterious **monastic islands** (p216)
🕐 1-2 days

Discover painted walls and links to *Titanic* in **Belfast** (p210)
🕐 1-2 days

Atlantic Ocean

Portballintrae

Coleraine

Lough Foyle

Waterfoot

Carnlough Bay

LONDONDERRY

ANTRIM

Derry/Londonderry

Ballymena

Larne

Bellaghy

George Best Belfast City Airport

Antrim

Belfast International Airport

Donegal

DONEGAL

BELFAST

Omagh

Cookstown

Lough Neagh

Lisburn

DOWN

Pettigo

Kesh

Lower Lough Erne

TYRONE

FERMANAGH

Upper Lough Erne

MONAGHAN

JONATHAN ARBUTHNOT/SHUTTERSTOCK ©
PAUL J MARTIN/SHUTTERSTOCK ©

Practicalities

ARRIVING

Belfast International Airport Express buses run to Europa Bus Centre (30 to 55 minutes).

George Best Belfast City Airport Buses run to the city centre (15 minutes).

CONNECT

3G, 4G and 5G mobile broadband coverage is good in towns and cities, but patchy in remote rural areas.

MONEY

Northern Ireland uses sterling. Card payments are widely accepted. County Donegal, in the Republic, uses euros.

WHERE TO STAY

Place	Pro/Con
Belfast	Options at all price points, excellent transport links and close to nightlife; can be noisy.
Derry	Good for culture vultures and convenient for the Causeway Coast.
Newcastle	Hikers' hostels, scenic campsites and B&Bs close to the Mournes; inconvenient for exploring the north and west.

EATING & DRINKING

Ulster fry This greasy plate of sausages, bacon, eggs, potato bread, soda bread and tomato is the ultimate hangover cure.

St George's Market This Belfast market sells locally grown and artisan produce, including traditional baked goods, fresh fish, and meats and cheeses from nearby farms.

Must-try tipple
Boatyard double gin (p218)

Best fish and chips
Morton's (p234)

GETTING AROUND

Car The easiest way to get around. Roads are good and traffic is rarely a problem.

Bus Serve urban areas and connect the province's main towns, with less frequent services to most rural villages.

Train Link some towns to Belfast.

JAN - MAR
Cool weather, some sunshine and rain.

APR - JUN
Generally mild and occasionally hot; head to the coast.

JUL - SEP
Lingering warmer weather; don't miss the autumn leaves.

OCT - DEC
Days are short and chilly; time to get cosy.

31 Belfast's Painted **WALLS**

MURALS | STREET ART | CULTURE

Belfast has a tradition of painting walls that stretches back over 100 years. Murals on the gable ends of terraced houses have been used as a form of protest, to communicate messages directed at the local community or outsiders – and to mark out territory. Recently, a thriving street-art scene has emerged that steers clear of sectarian imagery.

© 4H4 PHOTOGRAPHY/SHUTTERSTOCK ©

🗺 **How to**

Getting around From Donegall Sq, the Glider G1 bus travels west up Divis St and Falls Rd and east up Albertbridge Rd to Connswater.

Wet-weather option Informative black taxi tours of the West Belfast murals can be booked at the Visit Belfast office on Donegall Sq N.

Guides Learn about the street art on a guided walking tour or check out the map showing street-art locations (seedheadarts.com).

VANDERWOLF IMAGES/SHUTTERSTOCK ©

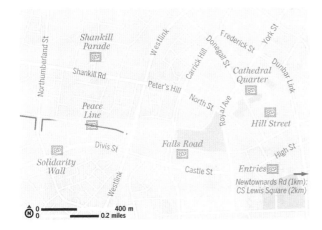

Far left top Cathedral Quarter tile mural map Far left bottom Political mural, Falls Rd

Murals & Street Art

Republican murals West Belfast is the best place to see the political murals the city is known for. Start with the international themes of the Solidarity Wall on Divis St and head west along Falls Rd towards Cultúrlann McAdam Ó Fiaich cafe and cultural centre (culturlann.ie), passing various murals including a tribute to hunger striker Bobby Sands.

Loyalist murals A Peace Line covered with murals and graffiti separates the Catholic community of the Falls Rd and the Protestant community of the Shankill; the gate on N Howard St is open during the day. Head to Shankill Parade to see King William III on his white horse and other Loyalist murals. The area is best avoided at night.

Street art Over the past 10 years, buildings in the Cathedral Quarter and the city centre have become a canvas for the work of local and international street artists. Keep an eye out for pieces as you walk around, and don't miss Hill St. 'Belfast is fertile ground for street art,' says Adam Turkington of arts and events company Seedhead Arts. 'Everybody in this city viscerally understands the importance of writing on walls, so when the street art movement starts and people see things on walls that are not divisive or oppressive, they immediately understand how positive that is and they celebrate it. It's about beautifying the place.'

Belfast's Best Works

Cathedral Quarter *Son of Protagoras* is incredible and *Dance by Candlelight, the Duel of Belfast* is the most iconic piece in the city. The annual street art festival **Hit the North** is held on the block around Belfast's best pub, the Sunflower (sunflower belfast.com).

The Entries A series of murals inspired by the history of the entries (narrow alleyways) and the anti-establishment movements that bubbled up there.

East Belfast Walk up Newtownards Rd to CS Lewis Sq to see a number of pieces, including *Linenopolis* and the works at Vault Artists Studios (vaultartiststudios.com).

Recommended by Adam Turkington, creative producer from Belfast @ SeedheadArts

MURALS &
Street Art

01 Solidarity Murals
Republican sympathy with international causes is frequently expressed in murals, such as this Solidarity POWs mural by Danny Devenny and Carlos Latuff.

02 Bobby Sands
Several murals in West Belfast commemorate the Hunger Strike of 1981. Among them is this image of Bobby Sands on Falls Rd.

03 Titanic, Ship of Dreams
In the shadow of the Harland and Wolff shipyard cranes, this mural on Newtownards Rd recognises the importance of the shipbuilding industry in East Belfast.

04 Dance by Candlelight
Two men fight over a dead animal as the world collapses in Conor Harrington's *Dance by Candlelight, the Duel of Belfast*.

05 The Son of Protagoras
Opposite Belfast's St Anne's Cathedral is MTO's image of a boy holding the dove of peace that has been killed by the twin arrows of religion.

06 Linenopolis
On the Newtownards Rd, Nomad Clan's

piece shows a woman surrounded by flax flowers, a reference to the linen industry.

07 Peace Mural
The 12 murals painted by the Bogside Artists of Derry between 1994 and 2006 are collectively known as the People's Gallery.

08 Death of Innocence
The Bogside Artists' Derry portrait of Annette McGavigan, who was killed aged 14 in 1971, represents all the children killed during the Troubles.

09 The Petrol Bomber
Another People's Gallery mural in Derry depicts a young boy holding a petrol bomb during the Battle of the Bogside in 1969.

10 Bloody Sunday
Here the Bogside Artists depict a group of men carrying the body of Jackie Duddy led by local priest Father Daly, in Derry.

Titanic Belfast

THE CITY THAT BUILT THE INFAMOUS SHIP

Belfast's Harland and Wolff shipyard cranes loom over the site where RMS *Titanic* was built. Workers at the time were proud of their part in creating the world's most luxurious liner, and poignantly unaware of the tragedy that would unfold when the ship set sail in April 1912.

TAKASHI IMAGES/SHUTTERSTOCK ©

The synopsis of what happened to the *Titanic* is well known: a ship lauded as the world's biggest and best set off on its maiden voyage amid much fanfare. But on 14 April 1912, in the most notorious nautical disaster of all time, the *Titanic* struck an iceberg in the North Atlantic and sank in the early hours of the following day, resulting in the deaths of some 1500 passengers and crew (the exact figure is disputed). Official inquiries into the tragedy on both sides of the Atlantic did little to dispel speculation and debate about its causes. Public intrigue was compounded by the glamour of the rich passengers on board and the role of hubris in the ship's fate.

But what of the city where the *Titanic* was built? In the early 1900s transatlantic passenger liners vied for custom from wealthy travellers and people emigrating. In an attempt to outdo the competition, White Star chairman Bruce Ismay commissioned three luxury liners – designed for comfort rather than speed – to be constructed at Belfast's Harland and Wolff shipyard. In 1909 the keel for the *Titanic* was laid alongside sister ship *Olympic*. At that time Belfast was a shipbuilding powerhouse, and Harland and Wolff employed around 14,000 people to work on the liners.

Susie Millar's great-grandfather, Tommy Millar, worked in the Harland and Wolff engine room and later joined the *Titanic's* crew as a deck engineer. He didn't survive the voyage, leaving two young sons behind in Belfast. Their story forms part of her *Titanic*-themed tours of the city (titanictours-belfast.co.uk).

'When I was growing up in Belfast, the *Titanic* wasn't much discussed,' says Millar. 'Talking about it was seen as

Left and middle Titanic Belfast museum **Right** SS Nomadic

bad form or bad luck, even in my family where my father had lost his grandfather. I knew the story because when I was eight years old I was given a book to read which my grandfather had written, about his father sailing away on *Titanic*, and what had happened to him. I knew my great-grandfather's name was on the Titanic Memorial at City Hall but the anniversary wasn't commemorated here in Belfast.'

'Talking about it was seen as bad form or bad luck, even in my family where my father had lost his grandfather.'

Regeneration

The turning point came in the 1990s, when – partly prompted by the 1997 release of James Cameron's movie – there was renewed interest in the *Titanic*. 'People were coming to Belfast and trying to find where the *Titanic* had been built and there was nothing; they were wandering across wastelands,' says Millar. 'As we came out of the Troubles and were moving towards the centenary of *Titanic* in 2012, there was a realisation that we needed to have some kind of interpretation here of the back story of the ship.'

Since 2009, the former shipyards have been transformed into the Titanic Quarter as part of a multimillion-pound regeneration project. At its centre is the multimedia museum Titanic Belfast, which opened in 2012.

'I love standing on the slipway and imagining the *Titanic* leaving with just a few people on board,' says Millar. 'There's so much connected to *Titanic* in Belfast that's authentic.'

⚓ Best Titanic Sights

Titanic Belfast The multisensory, multimedia extravaganza at the heart of Belfast's Titanic Quarter (titanicbelfast.com).

SS Nomadic The White Star steamship that ferried passengers to *Titanic* from Cherbourg Harbour (nomad icbelfast.com).

Slipways Behind the gleaming edifice of Titanic Belfast are the slipways where *Titanic* and *Olympic* were built.

Harland and Wolff Drawing Offices The designs for *Titanic* were drawn up in these offices, now part of Titanic Hotel (titanichotel belfast.com).

Titanic's Dock and Pump-House *Titanic* was fitted out in the vast Thompson Graving Dock (titanicsdock.com).

Titanic Memorial Monument and Garden In the grounds of Belfast City Hall.

32 Fermanagh's
LAKELANDS

ISLANDS | WATER SPORTS | WILDLIFE

▬▬▬ Once home to monasteries that were leading centres of learning and innovation, the islands of Lough Erne are now occupied mostly by birds and livestock. The spiritual legacy and enduring mystery of the islands hangs like mist over the water.

How to

Getting here Express buses connect Enniskillen with Belfast (130km) and Dublin (180km), but local bus services around Lough Erne are limited.

Boat trips Ferries to Devenish Island depart from Trory jetty; the White Island ferry leaves from Castle Archdale marina (castle archdaleboathire. com). Erne Water Taxi (ernewatertaxi.com) provides transport anywhere on the lough. In Enniskillen, Erne Tours (ernetours.com) offers trips to Devenish Island and Erne Boat Hire (erneboathireltd.com) has self-drive rentals.

SCENICIRELAND.COM/CHRISTOPHER HILL PHOTOGRAPHIC/ALAMY STOCK PHOTO ©

Exploring Lough Erne

Unique landscape Upper and Lower Lough Erne – two freshwater lakes linked by a river – comprise a mesmerising landscape of snaking waterways and hidden bays. The lough is dotted with 154 islands, or drumlins: little hills formed during the last glacial period, that are best viewed from the water. As little as 100 years ago these drumlins were home to a community of some 500 islanders; now all but two of the islands are uninhabited. 'When you're sitting in the middle of the lake, you can hear nothing but the sound of birds and water lapping against the side of the boat,' says Barry Flanagan, a local water taxi tour operator.

On the water Options for water sports abound, from stand-up paddleboarding, canoeing and kayaking to self-drive motorboats and hydrobikes. Equipment hire is available at

JE VEEN/500PX/GETTY IMAGES ©

Wildlife Watch

The woodlands, meadows and parkland of **Crom** (nationaltrust.org.uk/crom), on the shores of Upper Lough Erne, are home to red squirrels, otters, pine martens and rare species of butterfly. The Lower Lough is an important area for curlews, lapwings, snipe and breeding sandwich terns. Look out for kingfishers, too.

Left Common curlew **Above left** Lough Erne islands **Above right** Monastery ruins. Devenish Island (p218)

the Enniskillen Blueway Water Activity Zone, Castle Archdale marina and Share Discovery Village. 'You can easily canoe from Enniskillen to Devenish Island, which is a lovely half-day paddle, with the option of going with a guide,' says Flanagan. 'Upper Lough Erne is another fantastic place to go canoeing and kayaking. It's quite sheltered because the islands are all quite close together. You can go from Share Discovery Village all the way down to Crom.'

Island temple Flanagan also recommends the Hare Krishna temple (krishnaisland.org) on the island of Inish Rath. A ferry service operates on Sundays, when the temple is open to visitors.

Holy Islands

Monastery On **Devenish Island**, the remains of a 6th-century Augustinian monastery, a near-perfect 12th-century round tower and a 15th-century high cross are the legacy of

ⓘ Local Tips

Favourite trail The trail through Ballintempo Forest to Aghanaglack Neolithic tomb; it's part of the Marble Arch Caves Global Geopark. Hiring an e-bike from Corralea Activity Centre (corralea.com) helps with the hills.

Escape the crowds Lough MacNean is completely untouched. Head out in a boat and you'll likely have the lake to yourself.

Local produce Fermanagh Black Bacon (blackbacon. com) – the pigs are reared on Inishcorkish Island – plus sourdough bread from Joe the Baker (joethebaker. com), and Boatyard gin (boatyarddistillery.com) – its distillery tours get rave reviews.

Recommended by Barry Flanagan, owner of Erne Water Taxi in Enniskillen @ErneWaterTaxi

Left Lough MacNean **Below** Caldragh Graveyard, Boa Island

a once thriving monastic site where up to 1000 monks lived and worked. 'The buildings that remain help tell the story of what the monks' lives would have been like, the power they wielded and their importance in terms of the history of Ireland,' Flanagan explains. 'The place has remained unchanged for hundreds of years, and you really get a sense of its spiritualness. Walk through the gate behind the church; from the hilltop there is a great view of the whole island, down to the lake.'

Mysterious figures Within the ruins of a 12th-century church on **White Island** sit eight extraordinary stone figures, thought to date from the 9th century. Their age and interpretation is the subject of much debate. 'Little is known about their history, but the stones speak for themselves,' says Flanagan. On **Boa Island** (accessible by road) two intriguing stone figures sit in spooky Caldragh Graveyard. The larger is thought to date from the early Christian period and could represent the war goddess Badhbh from Irish mythology.

On Location

THE LASTING LEGACY OF GAME OF THRONES

If Ulster's rolling hills, damp forests and craggy coastline look familiar it may be because you've seen them on screen. Much of the blockbuster series *Game of Thrones* was filmed in Northern Ireland, with locals appearing as battle scene extras alongside Jon Snow.

Andrew McClay, a guide for Game of Thrones Tours in Belfast (gameofthronestours.com), has loved the George RR Martin books since he was 13, and appeared as an extra on *Game of Thrones*. 'I started growing a beard, and made myself look like I belonged in the show,' he recalls.

'My favourite episode to film was Battle of the Bastards, in Season 6. We had a training week and nobody knew what was happening, we were just being trained with swords, shields, bows and arrows. At the end of the week we found out it was Stark vs Bolton, and we had to line up to find out which we were. I thought, what am I going to do if they make me a Bolton? I can't put on that uniform,' says McClay, laughing, 'But I was house of Stark.'

He also worked in the costume department. 'They loved having me there because I knew every piece of armour in the show, and what belonged to who. So when I wasn't an extra I would be in scrubbing helmets. If I wasn't killing I was cleaning,' he says. One of McClay's filming areas was Magheramorne Quarry on the Antrim coast. 'We did a lot of battle stuff there, including filming for 55 nights for the Long Night in Season 8,' he says. Temperatures got as low as -12°C.

Now McClay uses his experiences on the show to inform his tours. 'When I was on set I would ask questions to people in production about how they did everything and what special techniques they used – the use of light to mimic the moon coming down into the cave and stuff like that.' Torn up paper was used as snow. 'The snow would be everywhere. They would turn on massive fans and then blow the snow so it exploded into a blizzard and we ran through it.'

Left Dark Hedges **Middle** Ballintoy Harbour **Right** Inch Abbey

The Thrones' Legacy

The filming of *Game of Thrones* is estimated to have brought £251 million to the local economy, and in 2019 the tourist board suggested that as many as 350,000 visitors per year had come to Northern Ireland just to visit filming locations used in the series.

Northern Ireland's film and TV industry also received a huge boost from *Game of Thrones* – the knowledge and experience gained from working on such a grand-scale production has prepared the local industry to host future blockbusters. Titanic Studios was recently used for the 2021 filming of *Dungeons & Dragons*, with Chris Pine, Regé-Jean Page and Hugh Grant, and a number of TV series have been filmed in Belfast, including the BBC series *Line of Duty*, which wrapped in 2020.

> The filming of *Game of Thrones* is estimated to have brought £251 million to the local economy

The success of *Game of Thrones* has helped rebrand Northern Ireland, show off its cinematic beauty and introduce it to a wider public. The area's popularity with Thrones fans looks likely to continue, with Linen Mill Studios (linenmillstudios. com) near Banbridge set to become a *Game of Thrones* studio tour.

Best Game of Thrones Locations

Castle Ward The estate was used as Winterfell in Season 1.

Tollymore Forest Park The direwolf cubs are found here.

Inch Abbey Robb Stark's camp in Season 1.

Cushendun Caves Where Melisandre gives birth to a shadow creature.

Ballintoy Harbour Lordsport on the Iron Island of Pyke, where Theon and Yara Greyjoy are reunited.

Larrybane Quarry Renly Baratheon's camp in Stormlands.

Dark Hedges These entwined beech trees are instantly recognisable as King's Rd.

Binevenagh The plateau was a filming location for the Dothraki grasslands in Season 5.

33 Heaney's HOMELAND

LITERATURE | CULTURE | LOUGHS

▬▬ Seamus Heaney's poetry is imbued with a sense of place and memories of the squelching bogs and blackberry picking of his childhood in rural County Derry. Near Heaney's first home, an exhibition at Seamus Heaney HomePlace highlights references in his poetry to the local landscape and real-life characters. In the surrounding countryside, the places that inspired Heaney wait to be explored.

🗺 How to

Getting here Bellaghy is an easy day trip by car from Belfast (53km) or Derry (62km) and driving is the best way to explore the surrounding countryside. Ulsterbus 212 Express from Belfast to Derry stops at Toomebridge (35 minutes) and Castledawson (45 minutes). From Castledawson, bus 127 towards Ballymena stops in Bellaghy (10 minutes), but buses are infrequent.

What to bring Collections of Heaney's poetry to read on location.

Left & Far left top Seamus Heaney HomePlace **Far left bottom** Church Island

Heaney's Inspiration

Culture fix A good place to start is Seamus Heaney Home-Place (seamusheaneyhome.com), an arts centre in the village of Bellaghy. The permanent exhibition here places Heaney's work in the context of his home and surroundings, with audio guides making it possible to hear the poems recited by Heaney himself. 'Don't miss Heaney's duffle coat and his old school bag,' says Eugene Kielt, a local tour guide.

Nearby, the sculpture *The Turfman* (2009) by David Annand is a visual representation of Heaney's poem 'Digging'. On the outskirts of Bellaghy village, Heaney's grave can be found at St Mary's Church.

Eel fishery 'Heaney wrote a number of poems about Toome-bridge and the eel fishery there, including "A Lough Neagh Se-quence", about the journey of the eels from the Sargasso Sea to Lough Neagh,' says Kielt. Across the bridge in Toome, a 2km walk leads along Toome canal to the shore of Lough Neagh.

Waterside 'Heaney's father used to raise cattle on a grassy area – or strand – between the road and Church Island on the western shore of Lough Beg,' Kielt explains. 'This tranquil place is the setting for the poem "The Strand at Lough Beg", dedicated to Heaney's cousin Colum McCartney, who was killed during the Troubles.' From the car park at Drumanee Rd a boardwalk leads to a wooded area, with views of Church Island.

 Around Castledawson

Moyola River This river flowed a few hundred yards from Mossbawn, the family farm where Heaney grew up. It's mentioned in 'Moyulla' and in his essay 'Something to Write Home About', in which he talks about crossing stepping stones. There's a riverside walk in Castledawson.

Lagans Road The country road that Heaney once walked down on his way to school – now named Creagh Hill – is referenced in a number of his poems. Stop for a drink at the **Old Thatch Inn** (oldthatchinn. com) and walk from there.

Recommended by Eugene Kielt, tour guide and B&B owner from Magherafelt (laurel-villa.com)

34 Hiking the **CAUSEWAY**

WALKING | LEGENDS | GEOLOGY

Uneven stacks of hexagonal basalt columns form a causeway into the ocean, an intriguing natural feature that legend says was the handiwork of giants. The Giant's Causeway is the area's star attraction — and deservedly so — but there's more to explore along this spectacular stretch of the north Antrim coast. So lace up your walking boots and follow our lead.

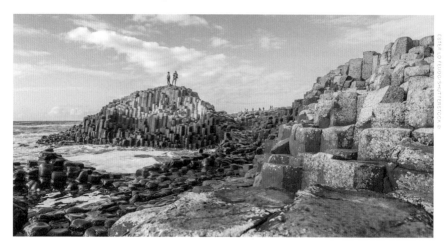

🗺 How to

Getting here/around
Buses and trains connect Belfast and Coleraine. Bus 172 and the seasonal Causeway Rambler service (April to September) run along the coast between Coleraine and Ballycastle.

When to go To avoid the summer crowds, visit in spring or autumn.

How much Visiting the Causeway is free. Park in Bushmills and take the bus to the Causeway to avoid paying the combined car park and visitor centre fee (adult/child £13/6.50).

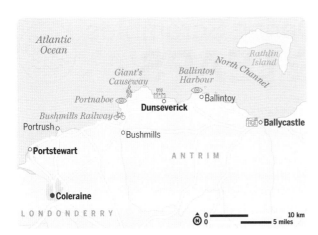

Causeway Walks

Causeway Coast Way This 50km walking trail from Portstewart to Ballycastle takes in dramatic cliffs, sandy beaches and castle ruins as well as the Giant's Causeway itself (walkni.com). The whole trail can be covered in two days, but the most stunning scenery is from Portballintrae to the Giant's Causeway (4.3km; an entirely off-road section taking in wild coastline), the Giant's Causeway to Dunseverick Castle (7.3km), and Dunseverick Castle to Ballintoy Harbour (7.8km; check the tide times to avoid high tide at White Park Bay).

'As you walk towards Dunseverick Castle, there's a bay called Port Moon and a little fisherman's bothy that sits in the bay. It's just the most amazing view when you come round the corner and look down,' says Mark Rodgers, a local guide. 'If you know what you're doing you can get down the pathway into Port Moon and you can actually stay in the bothy as well.' Contact the Causeway Coast Kayak Association (CCKA) for Port Moon bothy bookings.

Heritage railway A walking and cycling path runs alongside the tracks of the Giant's Causeway and Bushmills Railway, a seasonal, narrow-gauge railway, which follows the route of a 19th-century tourist tramway for 3km from Bushmills to the Giant's Causeway Visitor Experience. The walk crosses the River Bush and there are pretty views across the sand dunes.

Causeway trails Several waymarked trails lead directly to the stones or over the clifftops.

ⓘ Local Perspective

Favourite spot Portnaboe, which means 'Bay of Cows'. There's a real sense of calmness about it. Some of the fishermen and old guides who worked on the causeway had their ashes scattered there, and I feel very connected to that place.

Favourite time of year I like September and October. There's something very special about the colours at that time of year – the golds, browns and reds. The site's practically empty and you can watch the sunset at the Causeway with a drop of Bushmills whiskey.

Recommended by Mark Rodgers, a guide from Portrush (dalriadaking domtours.co.uk)

35

Daring Scrambles
& LEAPS

COASTEERING | ADVENTURE | MARINE LIFE

▬▬▬ The rugged shoreline of the Causeway Coast seems tailor-made for coasteering, an adrenaline-packed adventure activity that involves scrambling over basalt, swimming into sea caves, bobbing around on the swell in rock pools and jumping off sea stacks. It's an exhilarating way to explore this beautiful location, that even the less daring can enjoy. No previous experience or special skills required.

GARETH MCCORMACK/ALAMY STOCK PHOTO

🗺 How to

Where to do it Causeway Coasteering (causeway coasteering.com) in Portrush and Coasteering NI (coasteeringni.co.uk) in Ballintoy offer activities on the Causeway Coast.

When to go Summer offers calm, clear water and far-reaching views.

In autumn the sea is still warm. The churning winter seas and bracing winds appeal only to the super keen.

How much Around £40 per person for three hours, including winter wet suits, buoyancy aids and helmets.

STEPHEN BARNES/SPORT/ALAMY STOCK PHOTO

SHAWNWIL23/SHUTTERSTOCK ©

Left Kinbane Castle **Far left top** Coasteering group, Causeway Coast **Far left bottom** Wetsuits drying, Ballintoy

 Local Tips

Marine life We're always watching out for dolphins and porpoises, and we see seals quite a bit. Every now and then we spot basking sharks. I've never seen an orca, but they do occasionally visit here. There are also sea urchins and sea anemones.

Edible seaweed When we're out coasteering we nibble quite a few different types of seaweed. There's one that has a sort of garlicky, truffle taste, it's really surprising.

Local restaurant Native Seafood & Scran (nativeseafood.co.uk) in Coleraine. They're opening a restaurant in Portrush, too.

Recommended by Matt Wright of Causeway Coasteering (causewaycoasteering.com) in Portrush

Coastal locations A number of different locations are used for coasteering around the Causeway Coast. 'Each one has its own particular charm,' says Matt Wright of Causeway Coasteering. 'There are beautiful limestone caves around Whiterocks, and we go to a spot near Dunluce Castle. The headland at Runkerry is exceptional – there are three massive caves there – but it's an exposed area so we only go there when there's no swell. And occasionally we use Ballintoy, Portbradden and Kinbane Castle.'

Coasteering 'We start with some small jumps and as the session goes on the jumps will get higher – possibly as high as 12m, but not everybody does those,' says Wright. 'If there's a bit of swell in the water, which there usually is on the north coast, the whole coastline comes alive with waves washing up and down the rocks, creating pools where the waves wash in and then suck back out again.'

The activity also involves low-level rock climbing and scrambling. 'There are no harnesses involved. You're never really more than your own body height above the water,' says Bobby Marno, lead guide at Coasteering NI. 'There are days when the water's like glass. Standing on the top of the sea stacks, you can see clearly down to the seaweed and the sand on the bottom, and spot the odd dogfish or ray swimming about.'

36 Wild & Wonderful
DONEGAL

ATLANTIC COAST | REMOTE | ADVENTURE

With rugged coastal scenery, sandy beaches, inland forests and mountains, Donegal is the place to explore Ireland's wild side, to try new adventures and to experience the Atlantic Ocean's power. Explore the area by walking, driving the headlands, surfing or kayaking.

How to

Getting around
Explore by car or bike, so you can stop off for walks, picnics, photos and adventures.

When to go The best time to visit is between May and September, when everything is open. Weather can be unpredictable, so bring warm layers and a waterproof jacket.

Remote sleeps For unbeatable sea views, stay at a former lighthouse keeper's cottage such as Fanad Head or St John's Point (great lighthouses.com).

Coastal Headlands

With 1134km of coastline, at the start of Ireland's Wild Atlantic Way, Donegal has plenty of rugged headlands to drive, walk or climb, for the best Atlantic and coastal views. There are long, golden beaches too – perfect for walks, picnics, swimming or surfing.

Drive a loop of the Fanad Peninsula, passing Rathmullan, and walk the golden sands or picnic at **Ballymastocker Bay** or **Ballyhiernan Bay**, visiting Fanad Head for a tour of **Fanad Lighthouse**.

There's a bridge over to neighbouring Rosguill Peninsula – don't miss the 11km **Atlantic Drive** for stunning views of rocky headlands and beaches, perhaps stopping at Downings village, which overlooks Sheephaven Bay, for refreshments.

♪♪ Gaeltacht Culture

The Gaeltacht areas in Donegal, including on the islands, are where you will find the Irish language spoken and can experience traditional Irish culture like music, *sean-nós* ('old-style' songs) and dance. There are live traditional music sessions in many pubs and some areas have their own dance, such as the 'Waves of Tory' reel on Tory Island.

Left Malin Head (p230) **Above left** Fanad Lighthouse **Above right** St John's Point Lighthouse

On the Inishowen Peninsula, you can walk around **Malin Head**, Ireland's most northerly point, for sea air and views – if the landscape looks otherworldly, you might recognise it from some of *Star Wars: The Last Jedi*, which was filmed here as well as around Skellig Michael in Kerry (p168).

Atlantic Waves

If you really want to get up close and personal with the Wild Atlantic Way, take to the waves with a surf school or rent a board at beaches in Bundoran, Rossnowlagh and Dunfanaghy; jump into a sea kayak to marvel at caves and coves on the **Inishowen Peninsula** with Inish Adventures; or climb a sea stack with Unique Ascent.

Take a boat cruise on **Donegal Bay** or **Lough Swilly** sea inlet, or search for undersea shipwrecks on a diving trip with Mevagh Dive Centre. On land, you can try rock climbing, horse riding or cycling.

⚓ Donegal's Islands

Tory (Toraigh) Relaxed, rugged and remote – walk a loop along the cliffs and admire views of the mainland. Look out for puffins and seals. Don't miss the island's traditional music, singing, dancing and local myths and legends.

Arranmore (Árainn Mhór) Great for day trips or short breaks for nature hikes, fishing, cycling and kayaking. For beaches, try Aphort or Leabh Gharbh.

Gola (Oileán Ghabhla) Just 1km off the coast, with scattered old building remains. Try walking or birdwatching, visit sandy beaches like Tráigh na Béicí, or kayak or paddleboard with Gola Island Adventures.

Recommended by Henry Doohan, tour guide, donegaltourguide.ie @donegaltourguide

Left Tory Island ferry **Below** Mt Errigal

Wildlife Spotting

Glenveagh National Park covers 160 sq km and is a good place to spot wildlife – get a map and take one of the longer hikes away from the lake paths and you might spot some wild red deer. Look out for peregrine falcons and golden eagles, too.

You can also take a night-time walk with a bat detector, to observe signs of one of the many species of bat in the national park.

Off the coastal headlands of Donegal, dolphins, whales and basking sharks are often spotted, as well as seals. Seabirds like puffins, razorbills, fulmars and kittiwakes also arrive seasonally to breed – mostly in spring and summer.

Scenic Trails

For walking and hiking, Donegal is full of looped trails, through woodland and forest parks, along cliffs, beaches and shorelines.

If you have a head for heights, brave the narrow **One Man's Path** loop at Sliabh Liag for spectacular views down the 596m-high sea cliffs, or do an early morning climb to the top of **Mt Errigal** (751m). Both hikes take three to four hours each to complete.

For a gentler walk, take the lake paths at **Glenveagh National Park**, or the beach path at Ards Forest Park to enjoy a peaceful stroll along the dunes and boardwalk before exploring the forest trails on the way back.

DONEGAL'S
Favourite Beaches

01 Ballymastocker Bay

Beautiful long stretch of golden sand with scenic views from the Fanad Peninsula across Lough Swilly to the neighbouring Inishowen Peninsula.

02 Culdaff Beach

Sandy Blue Flag beach on the east side of the Inishowen Peninsula, with interesting rocky outcrops at one end.

03 Port Bán Beach

A beautiful sheltered white crescent beach near Dunree Head on Inishowen, reached by a grassy track.

04 Murvagh Beach

Near Rossnowlagh Beach and Donegal town, another Blue Flag spot, with dunes that lead in to Murvagh Forest.

05 Narin Beach

Sand dunes run along the back of this white sandy Blue Flag beach at Dunmore Head and its neighbouring beach at Portnoo.

06 Marble Hill Strand
Tucked away in Sheephaven Bay, this is a popular Blue Flag beach for holidaymakers in Dunfanaghy. The dunes are home to various wildflowers.

07 Rossnowlagh Beach
Stretching for 4km, with cliffs at one end, this beach is ideal for walking and is one of Donegal's best surf spots for beginners.

08 Kinnagoe Bay
A secluded beach on Inishowen that is sheltered by a hill. Just offshore, there's the shipwreck of a 1588 Spanish Armada ship.

09 Drumnatinny Beach
Walk through the dunes to reach this lovely long stretch of sand behind Falcarragh village, known locally as the 'back strand'.

Listings

BEST OF THE REST

Cliffs & Caves

Gobbins

An exhilarating guided walk along a cliff path, which involves navigating through a series of tubular bridges, tunnels and caves. It's in Islandmagee in County Antrim.

Carrick-a-Rede Rope Bridge

This narrow rope bridge spans the 20m-chasm between sea cliffs and a small island, near Ballycastle on the north Antrim coast.

Marble Arch Caves

A tour of these subterranean caverns includes a boat trip along an underwater river to view the picturesque formations of the Calcite Cradle. Near Enniskillen in County Fermanagh.

Green Spaces

Tollymore Forest Park

This scenic forest park near Newcastle offers fabulous walks and bike rides along the River Shimna and across the northern slopes of the Mourne Mountains.

Cave Hill Country Park

Waymarked trails lead to the summit of this north Belfast landmark; the view takes in the city, Belfast Lough and the Mourne Mountains.

Slieve Gullion Forest Park

In south Armagh, this forest park has an excellent children's adventure playground and storybook trail. A scenic drive leads to the starting point for a hike up Slieve Gullion (573m).

Botanic Gardens

The showpiece at this pretty Belfast park is the magnificent Palm House greenhouse, a masterpiece in cast iron and curvilinear glass.

Kilbroney Park

The views over Carlingford Lough from Rostrevor forest are simply spectacular. The region's best downhill mountain-biking trails can be found here, too.

Hill Climbs

Slieve Donard

The Mourne Mountains' highest peak (853m) is a straightforward climb, with far-reaching views from the top.

Ciulcagh Mountain

A boardwalk over blanket bog forms part of the trail up Fermanagh's highest hill (666m). The final ascent involves climbing stairs.

Slemish Mountain

Near Ballymena in County Antrim is the distinctive hill (438m) where a young St Patrick is said to have worked as a shepherd.

Waterside Bites

Morton's Fish & Chips £

Boats unload the daily catch of cod, haddock, scallops and scampi right alongside this harbourside hut in Ballycastle.

Pyke 'n' Pommes POD £

Locally sourced street food – tacos with Tequila-battered haddock, Porter-braised brisket or battered cauliflower; Wagyu beef burgers – served at a riverside shipping container in Derry.

Brunel's £££

On the Newcastle seafront in County Down, chef Paul Cunningham offers bold, creative and beautifully presented plates starring local ingredients.

Whiskey

Old Bushmills Distillery

Tours of the world's oldest licensed distillery include a sample of Bushmills whiskey, made with Irish barley and water from a tributary of the River Bush.

Pints & Trad Sessions

Leo's Tavern

The live sessions at Leo's are legendary, with musicians performing nightly during the summer and regularly throughout the year. It's in the Gaeltacht district of Gweedore in County Donegal.

Crawford's Bar

The County Down village of Rostrevor is known for its folk music; the Fiddler's Green International Festival is held here in July. Crawford's Bar hosts regular sessions and stocks local craft beers and spirits.

Culture

Ulster Museum

Highlights here include the Armada Room, with artefacts retrieved from the 1588 wreck of the Spanish galleon *Girona*, and the 2500-year-old Egyptian mummy Takabuti. Located in Belfast's Queen's Quarter.

Ulster American Folk Park

This open-air museum in County Tyrone tells the story of emigration from Ulster to America, recreating life on both sides of the Atlantic with original Irish cottages and New England log cabins.

Tower Museum

Inside a replica 16th-century tower house in Derry, this museum has exhibitions on the Armada shipwreck and the story of Derry, from St Colmcille to the Battle of the Bogside.

Dunluce Castle

St Patrick Centre

In Downpatrick, near St Patrick's grave, the *Ego Partricus*' (I am Patrick) multimedia exhibition tells the story of the saint's life.

Glebe Gallery

The late artist Derek Hill's Donegal home is filled with works by Tory Island artists as well as pieces by Picasso, Hokusai and Kokoshka. Lush gardens, too.

Castles & Country Houses

Dunluce Castle

The atmospheric ruins of Dunluce Castle sit perched atop basalt cliffs in County Antrim. The oldest parts date back to 1480.

Florence Court

Set in expansive gardens and wooded grounds, with 15km of walking and cycling trails, this grand property near Enniskillen is known for its rococo plasterwork and antique furniture.

Castle Ward

On the shores of Strangford Lough sits this grand house with an unusual quirk: the front-facing facade is neoclassical to please Lord Bangor, while the rear facade is Gothic to please his wife.

Scan for things to see, do and try in Ulster

Practicalities

ARRIVING

238

GETTING AROUND

240

SAFE TRAVEL

242

MONEY

243

RESPONSIBLE TRAVEL

244

ACCOMMODATION

246

ESSENTIALS

248

LANGUAGE

250

Right Dunquin, Dingle Peninsula (p153)

EASY STEPS FROM THE AIRPORT TO THE CITY CENTRE

Dublin is the primary point of entry for most visitors to Ireland. Located 13km north of the city centre, the airport has two terminals: most international flights (including most US flights) use Terminal 2; Ryanair and select others use Terminal 1. Both terminals have the usual selection of pubs, restaurants, shops, ATMs and car hire desks. You can also fly into Shannon or Belfast.

AT THE AIRPORT

SKÓRZEWIAK/SHUTTERSTOCK ©

SIM cards Can be purchased for unlocked phones from the SimLocal stands or vending machines in WHSmith (Terminal 1 Arrivals), Wrights (between Terminal 1 and 2) and Spar (Terminal 2). Shops are open 6am to 10pm every day and vending machines are accessible 24/7.

International Currency Exchange ICE outlets are located in Terminal 1 Arrivals (5.30am to midnight) and baggage hall (7am to 7pm) and Terminal 2 baggage hall (4.30am to 10.30pm). Rates are better at banks in the city.

WI-FI
Free unlimited wi-fi is available throughout Terminals 1 and 2. Select the Dublin Airport Wi-Fi network.

ATMS
Machins linked to Cirrus, Maestro or Plus are available in Terminals 1 and 2.

CHARGING STATIONS
Available in the seating areas of airside Departures, but not in Arrivals.

CUSTOMS REGULATIONS
Duty-free For duty-free goods from outside the EU, limits include 200 cigarettes, 1L of spirits or 2L of wine, 60mL of perfume and 250mL of eau de toilette.

Tax and duty paid Amounts that officially constitute personal use include 3200 cigarettes (or 3kg of tobacco) and either 10L of spirits, 90L of still wine or 110L of beer.

GETTING TO THE CITY CENTRE

HOW MUCH FOR A

Taxi
€25-30
45min

Dublin Bus
€3.30
45-60min

Aircoach
€7
30-60min

Aircoach offers three routes to more than 20 city destinations. The Aircoach stop is at zone 11 in Terminal 1, a two-minute walk from the Arrivals area at Terminal 1. Purchase tickets from staff at the bus stops or from the driver using cash or contactless payment.

Airlink Express Coach operates two routes, the 747 to Heuston Rail Station and the 757 to Camden St. Pick up is directly outside the Arrivals halls of Terminals 1 and 2. Pay with exact cash or use a Leap card.

Local Dublin buses 16, 41 and 102 all run to various points in the city centre. Bus stops are on the far side of the car park outside Terminal 1. Pay with exact cash or use a Leap card. Space for luggage is limited.

Taxi
The pick-up areas are directly outside the Arrivals concourse of both terminals. Note that not all taxis accept credit cards.

Plan Your Journey
Download the National Journey Planner app to figure out the most convenient way to get wherever you want to go in the city.

Visitor Leap Card
Purchase from the Bus & Travel Information Desk (Terminal 1 Arrivals) for unlimited travel on Dublin Bus (including Airlink airport bus services), Luas and DART.

Choose from 1/3/7 days for €10/19.50/40.

Top-up with additional time periods (1, 3, or 7 days) at any Leap outlet.

OTHER POINTS OF ENTRY

Inbound ferries arrive at the Dublin Port Terminal and are met by timed, express bus services that run to Westmoreland St in the city centre. Sail & Rail routes between Dublin and London allow travellers to combine bus, ferry and train tickets for as little as €35 one way.

Car ferries to Belfast from Liverpool (England) and Cairnryan (Scotland) dock at Victoria Terminal, while services from the Isle of Man arrive at Albert Quay. Both docks are less than 5km from the city centre and shuttles are available for foot passengers.

Belfast's International Airport is 30km northwest of the city. Taxis pick-up outside the Arrivals gate. Expect to pay around £25; it takes 20 to 40 minutes. Buy tickets from the machines at the stops before boarding Metro or Glider buses to the city centre.

Shannon Airport in County Clare is a one-hour drive from Galway City by car. It services numerous airport in North America and has US pre-clearance facilities.

TRANSPORT TIPS TO HELP YOU GET AROUND

The best way to explore Ireland is by car, which allows you to travel at your own pace and stop at scenic spots. Public transport between major urban centres is efficient and reasonably priced, and smaller towns and villages along those routes are well served. However, services to destinations not on major routes are less frequent and often impractical.

CAR

Driving is the most convenient way to explore Ireland and cars can be hired in every major town and city. Most cars are manual; automatic cars are more expensive. If driving into Northern Ireland make sure your insurance covers journeys to the North.

BUS

Buses are the most cost-effective way to get around. Private bus companies compete with Bus Éireann in the Republic and also run where the national buses are irregular or absent. Ulsterbus operates routes in Northern Ireland.

CAR RENTAL PER DAY

from €15

Petrol approx €1.43/litre

Tolls €1.40 to €3.10

BOAT

Boats serve Ireland's offshore islands. Ferries also operate across rivers, inlets and loughs, providing useful shortcuts, particularly for cyclists. Scenic cruises operate on many of Ireland's loughs and waterways.

TRAIN

Ireland's rail network is limited but trains are a quick and comfortable option for certain intercity routes, including Belfast to Dublin and Dublin to Cork. Services are operated by Iarnród Éireann (Irish Rail) in the Republic and NI Railways in Northern Ireland. For the best fares, book in advance.

DRIVING ESSENTIALS

 Drive on the left, overtake on the right. At roundabouts, give way to the right.

 Drivers must be at least 17 years old.

 The speed limit is 120km/h on motorways (70mph in Northern Ireland); 50km/h (30mph in Northern Ireland) in urban areas unless otherwise stated.

 The legal alcohol limit is 50mg of alcohol per 100ml of blood.

Ireland's rural roads can be steep, narrow and winding. Single-track roads with blind bends can be challenging, even without the hazard of wandering sheep. If you see an oncoming car look for a passing place to pull into; the etiquette is for the car nearest to a passing place to reverse (thank the driver with a wave). Be aware that in the hills mist can roll in quickly, leading to poor visibility.

CYCLING

Ireland's compact size and scenic landscape makes cycling an appealing way to get around. The downsides are unreliable weather and narrow country roads. A network of signed, off-road and low-traffic cycle routes is being developed and includes several 'greenways' along former railway tracks. Bike rental is readily available in tourist centres. There are bike-share schemes in Dublin and Belfast.

TOLLS

Charged on several motorways, usually by machine or booth. The M50 uses barrier-free electronic tolling, which uses cameras to record vehicle number plates. Pay tolls online by 8pm the following day. Some car rental companies include tolls in the fee.

SCENIC ROUTES

If you're driving, get off the main roads when you can: some of Ireland's most stunning scenery is best enjoyed on the secondary or tertiary roads that wind their way through standout photo ops.

KNOW YOUR CARBON FOOTPRINT

Driving from Dublin to Cork would emit about 50kg of carbon dioxide. A bus would emit 26kg for the same distance, per passenger. A train would emit about 10kg.

There are a number of carbon calculators online that allow you to estimate the carbon emissions generated by your journey.

ROAD DISTANCE CHART (KM)

	Belfast	Cork	Dublin	Enniskillen	Galway	Kilkenny	Killarney	Sligo	Waterford	Wexford
Belfast	–									
Cork	424	–								
Dublin	167	256	–							
Enniskillen	133	355	162	–						
Galway	306	209	212	180	–					
Kilkenny	284	148	114	236	172	–				
Killarney	436	87	304	372	193	198	–			
Sligo	206	336	214	67	138	245	343	–		
Waterford	333	126	163	319	220	48	193	293	–	
Wexford	309	187	135	302	253	80	254	307	61	–

DANGERS, ANNOYANCES & SAFETY

Ireland is safer for travellers than most countries in Europe, but it's wise to keep up the same level of caution as you would back home. Luckily, natural disasters are extremely rare, and the island is even free of snakes.

THEFT & FRAUD

Don't leave anything visible in your car when you park. Skimming at ATMs can be a problem: watch out for machines that have been tampered with and be sure to cover the keypad with your hand when you input your PIN.

IRISH TOURIST ASSISTANCE SERVICES

ITAS (itas.ie) provides help and support to people who are victims of crime while travelling in Ireland. The best place to report a crime is the nearest Garda (police) station (PSNI station in Northern Ireland). Ask for an incident report, usually required for insurance claims and emergency travel documents.

NORTHERN IRELAND

Sectarian tensions don't often cause problems for visitors these days, but keep an eye on the news and avoid any areas where riots or clashes might occur. Bear in mind that religion and politics can be touchy topics of conversation. It's best to avoid Northern Ireland during the Orange Order parades of 12 July, when tensions run high.

MIDGES

These annoying little biting insects are most active between May and September, particularly in the boggy areas of Connemara and Donegal, and often appear in swarms around dusk. Luckily, they don't carry diseases.

STEFANIE MUELLER/SHUTTERSTOCK ©

PHARMACIES

For minor, self-limiting illnesses, pharmacists can give valuable advice and sell over-the-counter medication. They can also advise when more specialised help is required.

CAAMALF/SHUTTERSTOCK ©

LEGAL MATTERS

Possession of a small amount of cannabis usually attracts a caution; other drugs are treated more seriously. If you are arrested, you have the right to contact a lawyer or your embassy.

INSURANCE

EU citizens with a European Health Insurance Card (EHIC) are covered for most medical care in the Republic. In Northern Ireland everyone receives free emergency treatment at hospital accident and emergency (A&E) departments.

QUICK TIPS TO HELP YOU MANAGE YOUR MONEY

CREDIT CARDS

Visa and MasterCard credit and debit cards are widely accepted. American Express is only accepted by major chains. Chip-and-PIN is the norm for card transactions; the limit for contactless card payments is €50 (£45 in Northern Ireland). Smaller businesses prefer debit cards (and some will charge a fee for credit cards), and a small number of rural B&Bs only take cash.

CURRENCY

The Republic of Ireland uses the euro (€). Northern Ireland uses pounds sterling (£), though the euro is also accepted in many places.

CHANGING MONEY

The best exchange rates are at banks, though bureaux de change and other exchange facilities usually open for longer hours.

CURRENCY

Euro

HOW MUCH FOR A

Pint of Guinness
€5

Coffee
€3.50

Dinner for two
€40

ATMS

All banks have ATMs linked to international systems such as Cirrus, Maestro or Plus. Transactions incur currency-conversion fees, and credit cards can incur immediate cash-advance interest-rate charges.

TIPPING

Tipping 10% to 15% is customary in restaurants. Sometimes a service charge is added to the bill, in which case a further tip is not necessary. Tipping is not expected in pubs or bars.

EXCHANGE RATES

If offered a choice of currencies when paying by card, choose to pay in the local currency (euros in the Republic and pounds sterling in Northern Ireland) rather than your home currency.

TAXES & REFUNDS

In the Republic, most goods come with value-added tax (VAT) of 23%, which non-EU residents can claim back if the store in which the goods are purchased operates the Retail Export Scheme. In Northern Ireland the VAT rate is 20%. Non-EU and non-UK residents may be able to claim back VAT under the Tax-Free Shopping refund scheme. However, you cannot get a VAT refund if you travel from Northern Ireland to Britain, regardless of where you live.

DISCOUNTS & SAVINGS

Dublin Pass (dublinpass.com) Includes a hop-on, hop-off bus tour, free entry to 30 attractions and discounted entry to 20 more.

Heritage Card (heritageireland.ie) Includes free entry to all Office of Public Works–run heritage sites. It can be a good deal for families, depending on how many sites you plan to visit.

RESPONSIBLE TRAVEL

Tips to leave a lighter footprint, support local and have a positive impact on local communities.

ON THE ROAD

Look for companies that use smaller vehicles when taking tours to remote, rural areas. Large coaches can clog up narrow country roads.

Pay to use the car park at tourist spots and don't park on the roadside instead. Doing so can cause accidents and traffic delays.

Wild camping in camper vans is not permitted in Ireland. Ask the landowner's permission to stay overnight or find a legal stopover for your camper van on total campingireland.ie/legal-stopovers.

Sustainable Travel Ireland awards bronze, silver and gold certification to sustainable hotels, tour operators, attractions and restaurants. Certified businesses are listed on sustainabletravel ireland.ie.

Recycling is available for many forms of household waste, including plastic, cardboard and cans. Look for recycling bins in self-catering accommodation. Food waste is also separated from non-organic waste in most of Ireland. See mywaste.ie.

IRENE FOX/SHUTTERSTOCK ©

GIVE BACK

Clean up the coast Join a beach clean-up organised by Clean Coasts (cleancoasts.org).

Drop off any leftover supplies to food banks Many supermarkets have collection points for donated items near the tills. Donations of non-food items, such as toiletries and household cleaners, are also encouraged.

Food Cloud is a social enterprise that helps reduce food waste in Ireland. Volunteers can help with gleaning: collecting leftover crops from farmers' fields after the commercial harvest (food.cloud).

Find out the latest ways to take action for Irish wildlife or make a donation. The Irish Wildlife Trust campaigns for the continued protection of Ireland's wildlife and manages a number of wildlife reserves (iwt.ie).

LEAVE A SMALL FOOTPRINT

Stick to the trail when hiking. Be especially mindful not to stray off boardwalks, which are often constructed to protect Ireland's areas of blanket bog.

Carry reusable shopping bags. By law, Irish shops must charge for carrier bags, to encourage people to reuse them.

Many coffee shops offer discounts if you bring your own reusable cup.

Biodegradable waste can be harmful to wildlife and the local ecosystem – remember to dispose of it properly.

DOS & DON'TS

Do behave respectfully at national monuments and be sure not to climb on or deface ancient sites.

Don't bring up the subject of local politics or religion unless you are sure the topic won't cause offence, particularly in the North.

Do be sensitive and tactful when discussing Irish history.

SUPPORT LOCAL

Design Ireland highlights independent Irish designers and makers. Their handmade arts and crafts make perfect souvenirs (designireland.ie).
Craft NI does the same for Northern Ireland (craftni.org).
Eat locally. Buy fresh produce and artisan goods at local farmers markets and farm shops. The Irish Organic Association has a list of organic farm shops (irishorganicassociation.ie).

CLIMATE CHANGE & TRAVEL

It's impossible to ignore the impact we have when travelling, and the importance of making changes where we can. Lonely Planet urges all travellers to engage with their travel carbon footprint. There are many carbon calculators online that allow travellers to estimate the carbon emissions generated by their journey; try resurgence.org/resources/carbon-calculator.html. Many airlines and booking sites offer travellers the option of offsetting the impact of greenhouse gas emissions by contributing to climate-friendly initiatives around the world. We continue to offset the carbon footprint of all Lonely Planet staff travel, while recognising this is a mitigation more than a solution.

RESOURCES
iwt.ie
sustainabletravelireland.ie
npws.ie
supportlocalni.com

UNIQUE AND LOCAL WAYS TO STAY

Ireland has a range of accommodation options to suit every budget, from hiker hostels to family-run B&Bs and luxury hotels; look for rooms with views of Ireland's scenic landscape and coastline. Glamping has become popular in recent years, with timber pods offering protection against the rain.

HOW MUCH FOR A

Glamping pod €80

Castle hotel €180

Horse-drawn caravan €230

DESIGN PICS INC/ALAMY STOCK PHOTO ©

CASTLES, TOWERS & GATE LODGES

If the romantic in you dreams of staying in a castle, Ireland might be the place to live out your fantasies. Many of the country's historic castles are now hotels, and luxurious ones at that – check out Bally-nahinch Castle in Connemara, Belleek Castle in County Mayo and Lough Eske Castle in County Donegal. A number of castles, towers and gate lodges contain self-catering apartments available to rent as holiday lets; most are in su-perb locations with expansive manicured grounds.

CABIN CRUISERS & CANAL BARGES

A lovely way to explore Ireland's inland waterways is to hire a live-aboard motorboat or canal barge. The Shannon-Erne Waterway is a peaceful place for a barge holiday. In County Ferman-agh, a number of companies offer self-drive, liveaboard cabin cruisers for explor-ing Lough Erne. No previous boating experience is required.

PETER KROCKA/SHUTTERSTOCK ©

LIGHTHOUSES

Spectacular sea views, wild scenery and excellent birdwatching are just some of the advantages of spending the night in a lighthouse. Several light-houses in Ireland are available to rent as holiday lets, including the remote Fanad Head Light-house in Donegal, Wicklow Head Lighthouse, and St John's Point lough erne Lighthouse in County Down (greatlighthouses.com).

TREE HOUSES & FOREST BUBBLE DOMES

For something different, how about a night in the trees? Some are luxurious offerings with hot tubs and mod cons, while others are more basic. The transparent bubble domes at Finn Lough (finnlough.com) in Fermanagh make it possible to stargaze from bed. The domes are set in secluded woodland on the shores of Lough Erne.

HORSE-DRAWN CARAVAN

It's possible to hire a traditional, horse-drawn wagon, which you can drive around peaceful countryside and sleep in overnight. Caravans have gas-fired cooking facilities and gas lamps, but no electricity or bathrooms. Clissmann Horse Caravans (clissmannhorsecaravans.com) offer trips in County Wicklow.

GLAMPING PODS & YURTS

If Ireland's wet weather puts a dampener on the idea of a night under the canvas, a glamping pod might be the perfect alternative. These timber pods vary from bare-bones bunks (bring your own sleeping bag) to luxurious offerings with beds, cooking facilities and even bathrooms.

The best are positioned to make the most of their surroundings, and often offer outstanding views. A number of places in Ireland also offer overnight stays in yurts, often with wood-burning stoves, king-sized beds and furniture. Glamping is popular, so book well in advance.

BOOKING

Advance bookings are generally recommended and are an absolute necessity during the July and August holiday period. The summer public holidays are the first Monday in August in the Republic, and 12 July and the last Monday in August in the North.

Discover Ireland (discoverireland.ie) and **Discover Northern Ireland** (discovernorthernireland.com) have extensive accommodation listings. Local tourist information offices can often book accommodation on your behalf.

Daft.ie (daft.ie) Online property portal that includes holiday homes and short-term rentals.

Elegant Ireland (elegant.ie) Specialises in self-catering castles, period houses and unique properties.

Imagine Ireland (imagineireland.com) Holiday cottage rentals across Ireland.

Irish Landmark Trust (irishlandmark.com) Not-for-profit conservation group that rents self-catering properties of historical and cultural significance, such as castles, tower houses, gate lodges, schoolhouses and lighthouses.

National Trust (nationaltrust.org.uk) Self-catering cottages and campsites on National Trust properties in Northern Ireland.

Lonely Planet (lonelyplanet.com/ireland/hotels) Recommendations and bookings.

Dream Ireland (dreamireland.com) Lists self-catering holiday cottages and apartments.

VIKING HOUSE

Spend the night in a recreated Viking house from 1000 years ago, with wattle walls, a thatched roof and a central hearth. It's at the Irish National Heritage Park in County Wexford.

ESSENTIAL NUTS-AND-BOLTS

PUBLIC HOLIDAYS

Public holidays can cause road chaos as everyone tries to get away for the break. Book accommodation in advance.

CROSSING THE BORDER

There are no border checks between the Republic of Ireland and Northern Ireland.

SMOKING

Throughout Ireland smoking indoors is illegal everywhere except in private residences and designated hotel rooms. Smoking in cars carrying children is also illegal.

FAST FACTS

Time Zone
GMT+1

Country Code
+353

Electricity
230V/50Hz

GOOD TO KNOW

 Visas are not required by most citizens of Europe, Australia, New Zealand, USA and Canada.

 In case of emergency, dial 999 (police, fire and ambulance).

 The electricity supply is 230V/50Hz. Plug sockets are three-pronged (as in the UK).

 USB ports on plug sockets are increasingly common in hotels and cafes.

 Ireland uses the metric system, except for liquid measures of alcohol, where pints are used.

ACCESSIBLE TRAVEL

New buildings all have wheelchair access. Historic sites such as castles and towers may not have lifts.

Hotels often have lifts, ramps, hearing loops and rooms with accessible bathrooms. Disabled Friendly Hotels (disabledfriendlyhotels.com) has a database of accessible accommodations.

Parking bays for people with disabilities are generally available at shopping centres and other attractions.

City buses usually have low-floor access and priority spaces on board. Not all Bus Éireann Expressway and Regional services are wheelchair-accessible. Note that many rural bus stops are not accessible.

Useful resources include Accessible Ireland (accessibleireland.com) and AccessAble (for Northern Ireland; accessable.co.uk).

MOBILE PHONES
European phones work in Ireland. Check international phones are not locked to a local network.

PUB ROUNDS
In pubs it's usual to take turns to buy a round of drinks for the whole group.

GREETINGS
Shake hands and make eye contact when meeting for the first time and when saying goodbye.

FAMILY TRAVEL

Public transport is free for children under five.

Hotels can usually provide cots with advance notice. Some bigger hotels offer kids clubs during school holidays. Some B&Bs do not accept children.

Restaurants generally have high chairs, children's menus and baby-changing facilities. High-end restaurants may be unsuitable.

Pubs do not allow under-15s in after 9pm.

Visitor attractions nearly all cater to children and offer reduced-price tickets for kids and families.

TIME
In winter (November to March) Ireland is on Western European Time, also known as Greenwich Mean Time (GMT) or Universal Time Coordinated (UTC). In summer (April to October), clocks shift to GMT/UTC plus one hour, also known as Irish Standard Time (IST) or British Summer Time (BST).

BREXIT
As part of the treaty that took the UK out of the EU, the Northern Ireland Protocol guarantees an open border in Ireland, without additional border checks or formalities. This means Northern Ireland continues to follow many EU rules relating to imports and exports.

LGBTIQ+ TRAVELLERS
Although a generally tolerant place for LGBTIQ+ travellers, Ireland's LGBTIQ+ community continues to face discrimination and homophobic abuse.

Same-sex marriage has been legal since 2015 (2020 in Northern Ireland).

Well-established gay scenes exist in Dublin, Belfast, Galway and Cork. Pride is celebrated in all four cities.

Leo Varadkar, Taoiseach from 2017 to 2020, was Ireland's first openly gay head of government.

Gay Community News (GCN; gcn.ie) is a monthly magazine with local news and features.

LANGUAGE

Irish (Gaeilge) is the country's official language. Despite this, it is really only spoken in pockets of rural Ireland known as the Gaeltacht. Ask people outside the Gaeltacht if they can speak Irish and they will probably reply, 'ah, cúpla focal' (a couple of words). Irish divides vowels into long (those with an accent) and short (those without). Other than a few odd-looking clusters, such as **mh** and **bhf** (both pronounced as w), consonants are generally pronounced as they are in English.

BASICS

Hello.	Dia duit.	*deea gwit*
Goodbye.		
(when leaving)	Slán leat.	*slawn lyat*
(when staying)	Slán agat	*slawn agut*
Yes.	Tá.	*taw*
No.	Níl.	*neel*
Thank you (very much).		
	Go raibh (míle)	*goh rev (meela)*
	maith agat.	*mah agut*
Excuse me.		
	Gabh mo leithscéal.	*gamoh lesh scale*
Sorry.		
	Tá brón orm.	*taw brohn oruhm*
What's your name?		
	Cad is ainm duit?	*kod is anim dwit*
My name is ...		
	... is ainm dom.	*... is anim dohm*
Do you speak Irish?		
	An bhfuil Gaeilge agat?	*on wil gaylge oguh*
I don't understand.		
	Ní thuigim.	*nee higgim*

CÚPLA FOCAL

Tóg é go bogé.		
Take it easy.		*tohg ay go bogay*
Slainte!		
Your health!/Cheers!		*slawncha*
Nollaig shona!		
Happy Christmas!		*nuhlig hona*
Cáisc shona!		
Happy Easter!		*kawshk hona*
Go n-éirí an bóthar leat!		
Bon voyage!		*go nairee on bohhar lat*

1	haon	*hayin*	6	sé	*shay*
2	dó	*doe*	7	seacht	*shocked*
3	trí	*tree*	8	hocht	*hukt*
4	ceathaír	*kahirr*	9	naoi	*nay*
5	cúig	*kooig*	10	deich	*jeh*

SIGNS

Mna	*mnaw*	Women
Fir	*fear*	Men
Leithreas	*lehrass*	Toilet
Gardaí	*gardee*	Police
Oifig	*iffig*	Post
An Phoist	*ohn fwisht*	office

Index

000 Map pages

000 Map pages

NOELLE KELLY

Noelle is a travel writer, blogger and yoga teacher from Thurles, Co Tipperary. She enjoys travelling slowly, learning about new cultures, cuisines, and nuances of wherever she's exploring. When not on her yoga mat, Noelle shares her adventures on her website.

🖥 WanderingOn.com

My favourite experience is wandering around Cork City. I always end up in the English Market sampling the gastronomic delights.

FIONÁN MCGRATH

Irish-born, part-time Canadian, Fionán has lived in six countries and loves off-the-beaten-track travel activities especially wild camping and bike packing.

My favourite experience is bike packing around West Cork.

ORLA SMITH & NEIL ARTHURS

Dubliners, Neil and Orla, found they shared a love for travel and adventure when they met in Sydney back in 2004. Neil's skills as a professional photographer and Orla's passion for travel writing helps to keep them on the road.

My favourite experience Neil's favourite experience is capturing the Northern Lights in Iceland. Orla's is midnight swimming among bioluminescence in Lough Hyne in the south of Ireland.

THIS BOOK

Design development
Lauren Egan, Tina Garcia, Fergal Condon,

Content development
Anne Mason

Cartography development
Wayne Murphy, Katerina Pavkova

Production development
Mario D'Arco, Dan Moore, Sandie Kestell, Virginia Moreno, Juan Winata

Series development leadership
Liz Heynes, Darren O'Connell, Piers Pickard, Chris Zeiher

Commissioning Editor
Daniel Bolger, Fergus O'Shea

Product Editor
Amy Lynch

Book Designer
Fergal Condon

Assisting Book Designer
Ania Bartoszek

Assisting Editors
Lorna Parkes, Gabrielle Stefanos

Cover Researcher
Lauren Egan

Thanks Gwen Cotter, Sandie Kestell, John Taufa, Saralinda Turner

Our Writers

ISABEL ALBISTON

Born in London and raised near Belfast, Isabel returned to Ireland in 2018 after living in Australia, Argentina and Spain. Jobs have included writing for newspapers and magazines, working as a Buenos Aires tour guide, and contributing to 15 Lonely Planet guidebooks.

My favourite experience is hiking the Causeway Coast Way, taking a bracing dip in the sea, and eating local seafood in a pub overlooking the ocean.

BRIAN BARRY

Cork-native Brian is a travel writer, photographer and digital nomad who has explored more than fifty countries. An adventure sports enthusiast, lover of the outdoors and independent travel advocate, Brian prefers the road less travelled.

🖥 WanderingOn.com

My favourite experience is road-tripping around West Cork, enjoying the spectacular scenery, finding hidden beaches, and immersing yourself in the Irish outdoors.

YVONNE GORDON

Dubliner Yvonne Gordon is an award-winning travel writer and photographer, specialising in adventure travel and contributing to publications including *The Sunday Times*, *The Washington Post*, *Wanderlust*, BBC Travel and AFAR.com.

My favourite experience is exploring the wild, remote side of County Donegal – surfing the amazing beaches, kayaking under cliffs and hiking the headlands.

ÚNA-MINH KAVANAGH

Kerrywoman Úna-Minh is an Irish speaker and multimedia creator who edits the good news website WeAreIrish.ie. She's a live-streamer who broadcasts in Irish and English on Twitch (twitch.tv/yunitex).

🐦 @unaminhkavanagh
🎵 @unaminh

My favourite experience is being among Irish-speaking communities. The Kerry Gaeltacht is one of my top places to visit, particularly Baile na nGall village.